JOINING THE MODERN WORLD

Inside and Outside China

JOINING THE MODERN WORLD

Inside and Outside China

Wang Gungwu

East Asian Institute, National University of Singapore

SINGAPORE UNIVERSITY PRESS
NATIONAL UNIVERSITY OF SINGAPORE

World Scientific
Singapore • New Jersey • London • Hong Kong

46465498   8-7-01

Published by

Singapore University Press
Yusof Ishak House, National University of Singapore
31 Lower Kent Ridge Road, Singapore 119078

and

World Scientific Publishing Co. Pte. Ltd.
P O Box 128, Farrer Road, Singapore 912805
USA office: Suite 1B, 1060 Main Street, River Edge, NJ 07661
UK office: 57 Shelton Street, Covent Garden, London WC2H 9HE

British Library Cataloguing-in-Publication Data
A catalogue record for this book is available from the British Library.

JOINING THE MODERN WORLD:
Inside and Outside China

ISBN   981-02-4488-6

Printed in Singapore.

Contents

Preface   vii

Joining the Modern World   1

The Chinese Revolution and the Overseas Chinese   15

A Single Chinese Diaspora?   37

Hong Kong and an Ambivalent Modernity   71

The Shanghai-Hong Kong Linkage   83

Transforming the Trading Chinese   97

Chinese Values and Memories of Modern War   107

Modern Work Cultures and the Chinese   129

Index   151

Contents

Preface

In recent years, I have been impressed by the fresh efforts of Chinese people everywhere to try to be as modern as possible. At the same time, I am struck by the way the criteria of what is modern has been changing during the past century. The standards of modernity, often proclaimed as self-evidently universal, have been set by the successful countries and these standards have been rising as those countries grow richer and more powerful. Two consequences follow from this trend. The first is positive. The higher demands make the Chinese work harder to strive for that elusive modernity. Never having been afraid of hard work, most young Chinese are ready to meet that challenge. The other is negative. The Chinese people are beginning to feel a deep contradiction in this setting of standards. When China and other similarly poor countries were down, the standards were low or lowered and little was expected of their leaders and the people. But when there has been marked progress, as has happened in China during the past two decades, standards were lifted incrementally so that China seems always to be behind, with little chance of ever reaching the moving standards expected of it. Indeed, standards seemed invariably higher for the Chinese as if the successful states sought to hold a moral sword above Chinese heads indefinitely. In addition, what sounds like a school principal's tone at seeing a poor report card at the end of each year is deeply offensive.

The ongoing drama of Chinese people trying to be modern has also been enacted in different parts of the world. There are interesting differences among these Chinese depending on where they have been living. The general trend, however, is unmistakable. A great striving for betterment is supported by a strong capacity to adapt and change, and this is reflected in the way Chinese seize new opportunities when they occur. The essays collected in this volume try to capture these efforts both inside and outside China. Seven of them were first presented as occasional lectures, each covering changes during the past century and a half. The sixth, "Transforming the Trading Chinese", was written to describe a longer term development that is transforming Asia generally, but China most remarkably. Together, they offer small pieces of the mosaic that seeks to portray some aspects of the Chinese practising the art of *modernising*.

The question remains, will the people in China go on accepting their fate as that of Sisyphus, condemned to push that huge modern boulder up a hill that seems to get steeper whenever they get near the top? Or, will they conclude one day that the mythical hill was placed there to keep them inferior and thus stop worrying about it? The evidence is that, when standards of progress take a people's history and cultural values into account, they are better understood and more readily sought after by these people and, therefore, more likely to be achievable. When they do not and, instead, are relative to the specific kinds of progress achieved by a few countries through accumulated wealth and power, such applications of standards undermine the will to keep trying. I do not believe the Chinese people are easily discouraged. We simply have to look at their history over the past 140 years or so to see how resilient and hopeful they have been. But it is important that these efforts get the recognition they deserve, not as proof that universal criteria have been validated but as achievements of people who have fought adversity with determination against all odds.

Joining the Modern World*

I have been asked to consider where China stands today in her long transition to modern political and economic structures. The central theme here is that China has been trying to join the modern world for about 140 years. I ask the following questions. How far has it succeeded? Hasn't it arrived at that goal not just once but many times? What does success mean if that modern world has not been a single set of norms but a number of shifting norms?

The first step was taken in 1861 when the Qing court established the "office for the general management of affairs and trade with every country", better known in short as the *Zongli yamen*. This was equivalent to a ministry of foreign affairs, and represented the first time that the Chinese empire formally acknowledged all foreign countries as equals. You will note that this first step was taken on the eve of the inauguration of President Abraham Lincoln. At that time, China was already engrossed in

---

*This lecture was the opening lecture at a symposium entitled "Coping with China". It was organised by the Ethics and Public Policy Center and the Ronald Reagan Foundation in Washington, D.C. on 9 May 2000.

a sort of civil war — the Taiping rebellion — and was soon to face other rebellions, for example, the Nian and the White Lotus in North China. And, by the time President Lincoln declared all slaves to be free in late 1862, two major Muslim rebellions in both China's north-west and south-west border provinces were threatening the dynasty. Also, it was not until eight years after the Confederate Army of General Robert E. Lee surrendered and the Union was saved, that the Qing armies finally, in 1873, suppressed all the major rebellions that had been plaguing the empire.

Compared with the four years of the American Civil War, the Chinese fought their own internal wars for at least 25 years. Another major difference was that China's was not a citizens' war pitting 21 million people in the north against 9 million in the south, but a series of wars by ruling elites to hold down a population of 400 million. However, there were features that were more comparable. For example, the unity of the polity was preserved and law and order reestablished. The numbers of casualties for both countries were excessive, and, taken in proportion, the ferocity and destruction were equally horrendous.

I use this comparison to illustrate several points. Both countries were taught bitter lessons from their respective wars. While they treated these internal conflicts as dire warnings against division, there were great differences in what they learnt from these events. To the United States, the Civil War was the source of honour and achievement to the country's leaders, part of a continuing education in nation-building. To the Chinese, their series of wars aroused much more ambivalent feelings among the ruling classes. They led to relief that the Confucian state survived, but they also confirmed that deep social and political cleavages existed within the population. The cleavages not only ensured that foreign pressures could prevail and the imperial Confucian state would soon perish, but they also bedevilled successive regimes of China for the next century.

For example, the Taiping rebels left a bloody experience of emotional populism to be taken up by nationalist and communist revolutionaries alike during the 20th century. This populism was rooted in a tradition of peasant rebellion, but it was also externally inspired and that provided a lesson in modern people power that would not only challenge future leaders of China but also frighten the later elites of every political persuasion. As for the fierce suppression of the Muslims in Xinjiang, that had become more than the normal task of defending China's northern and western borders. The intervention of Anglo-Indian and Russian forces was part of the modern world that was confronting China. The actions of the Great Powers in Central Asia, threatening to repeat what they had done on the China coast, made the Chinese leaders understand even better that the concept of sovereignty as the basis of modern nationhood applied no less to its precarious overland borders.

At the same time, economic penetration by foreign powers of China's markets had begun through the treaty ports, notably Shanghai, Guangzhou and Tianjin. New generations of entrepreneurs, industrialists and financiers emerged from these points of penetration as well as students of science, law and management. A deeper modernisation of new elites had begun. This process was accompanied by large-scale migration of Chinese workers and traders, who left the China coast to join those sojourners who were already in Southeast Asia and to lead the exodus to the gold fields of north America and Australasia. Most of the people who went abroad were those who had long resented the Manchu-based regime in Beijing. The opening to the outside world gave them a chance to experience new ideas of modernity. They were deeply impressed by what they saw outside — industrial growth, naval power, banking and finance and the laws which were the foundations of western society. They also found that their great civilisation was no longer admired by Westerners, who felt racially and culturally superior to the Chinese. Their response to such stimuli was to develop a sense of Chineseness which they had not been conscious of before. This took shape at the end of the century, in most part ambiguous and inchoate, but nevertheless gathering strong emotions akin to modern national pride. It gathered force as the next generation fought to free themselves from both Manchu rule, now described as alien, and from an archaic Confucian state.

New identities as modern Chinese were thus shaped, accompanied by great expectations. The world outside taught them that such political consciousness would be followed by the creation of a united sovereign Chinese nation, one that would be able to take advantage of all the technologies and institutions that were being introduced. New attitudes towards radical change were needed, and those who had benefited from commercial intercourse with the more advanced capitalist world and from formal study abroad were keen for the country to adjust to such changes. For most of the 20th century, there was virtually no resistance to the idea that China had to modernise. Calls for modern schools and colleges, all using textbooks modelled on Europe, the US and Japan, were heard all over the country. If anything, young people vied to be the most progressive because that was the most patriotic thing to do. In the shadow of the Social Darwinist ideas prevalent among them, modernisation was the only way to save the country from being declared unfit to survive.

The first years of the new Chinese Republic coincided with another war, the Great War of 1914–1918. The global impact of that war took many forms. The carnage arising from fierce national rivalries among the European powers was eye-opening and turned many Chinese thinkers away from Western Europe as models of development, including that of liberal and democratic capitalism. These Chinese were not in doubt that China had joined the modern world. But they saw that they had to make choices as to which bits of that world they should learn most from. By calling their country a republic in 1911, they believed they were embarked on the road to transformation. Indeed, expectations were so high that many were impatient to get away from their own past, from anything that seemed to stand in the way of the thorough modernisation their country needed. Since the 1890s, many elite groups had debated the virtues of several models from the West and from Japan. We now know that no ideology seemed to have been too new and untried to be debated. But the First World War and its aftermath did give them pause and led ultimately to a narrowing of practical models for China to choose from.

Judgments about being modern were made largely on two grounds: that which provided the surest way to wealth and power, and that which most quickly and directly served the needs of "the people", a new liberating ideal about helping the downtrodden majority which, while initially a slogan taken from the West, found deep roots in parts of Chinese tradition. Both these grounds led the Chinese away from the incremental reforms needed to modernise commerce and industry and consolidate economic development in stages. Instead, they turned to two rival ideologies, both from the West, that promised swift results: the first being the nationalist models of Germany, Italy and Japan, and the other, the Russian revolution that gave life to international communism. I shall not dwell here on the well-told story of what led to the defensive war against Japan and the victory of the Chinese Communist Party. The eventful years from 1937 to 1949 have been written about by many historians and political analysts and the consequences are now obvious to all.

I have offered this background to the present position of China in order to underline two points. First, that the Chinese have tried to be modern, not too reluctantly but too often. They always tried too hard and too impatiently to find short cuts to restore China to the self-respect and dignity they believed only modernity could bring. Second, that they have learnt how dynamic the concept of modernity is and have now come to terms with the way the markers that define modernity are moved every now and then. When the norms are changed, usually because of the influence of the richest and strongest power or group of powers, China's large and cumbersome structures have found it difficult to adapt and cope with each major shift.

The efforts by China's elites to modernise quickly have brought them much pain and distress as the people struggled with supposedly universal ideals which were not fulfilled, and with imported institutions which often did not work. It cannot be denied that the highest ideals that led China to several revolutions have come from the modern West. Whether it was nationalism, socialism, capitalism, liberalism or communism, the idea of responsible elites saving or serving, enriching or empowering, the people had always sounded beautiful. There was probably little wrong with the abstract goals these Chinese aspired to. The means to achieve their objectives, however, proved to be far more difficult to agree on. Again and again, they failed to find the way to realise their aims. The institutions were often dysfunctional, many of the leaders were corrupt and, repeatedly, the country was too weak or disunited to deal with the external interventions or threats it had to face. One could provide a long list of reasons for failure over the past 140 years. Among those that stand out were the disjunction between ruling class aspirations and grassroots reality, the tendency for the Chinese elites to crave decisive success while standing on shifting sands.

Although the urge to be modern has been strong among generations of the educated classes of China, they have not succeeded in building the modernisation they wanted on the foundations of their ancient civilisation. Since the late 1970s, there has been a retreat from revolutionary modernism towards an untried transition from a planned economy. This phase of nation-building seeks to reconcile new economic and social experimentations with an historic pride in a Chinese identity. Some parts of the reforms have been spectacularly successful. Others have led to the rise of new elite groups, each with unprecedented interests to protect. These new groups in leadership positions have little of the old over-arching ideals to fight for. The authority of the ruling Communist Party has been eroded by a number of self-destructive internal conflicts and also by the systemic weaknesses of Stalinist-Maoist economics. Their position today can only be defended by their success in meeting the expectations of an increasingly literate and pluralist society.

The current ruling groups are still being formed on the basis of older elites coopting those who have responded successfully to the new opportunities brought about by the recent reforms. As they gain in confidence, they have devised ways to consolidate their power. These include learning from experiences elsewhere as well in history. For example, elites can be overthrown by their own people when they consistently fail to deliver on their promises. They can be removed by rebellions or revolutions, or through various kinds of democratic elections. By choosing the path of reform, the new leaders are trying to ensure that future developments will not encourage people to resort to violence again. They are fearful of losing what has been gained during the past 20 years and understandably wary about people power. Such power was harnessed by Mao Zedong, as well as by those who resisted him, to support the cause of fratricidal political struggles from the

Hundred Flowers campaigns through the Great Leap Forward to the Cultural Revolution. The destructive forces which those struggles unleashed have taught all Chinese to be shy of mass movements of any form.

The options open now include learning from recent Chinese history. China has always had powerful elites, and hard lessons have been learnt from earlier activist generations. For example, aristocrats and mandarins like Li Hongzhang and Zhang Zhidong, followed by militarists and warlords like Yuan Shikai and his officer class, who were then replaced by conservative nationalists of the Guomindang under Chiang Kai-shek and these in turn by the patriotic revolutionaries of Mao Zedong's Communist Party.

So what is different for the new leading groups today? As with similar groups in the past, their worlds have been challenged to change and prepare for more change. There was never a period that was stable for long. They had first believed that China's failures were largely due to not having enough moral and upright leaders and, therefore, a critical return to tradition was needed. Today, there are still echoes of that view, except that what is now regarded as their heritage includes, not only the surviving bits of Confucianism, Buddhism, Taoism and recently imported Christianity, but also what Mao Zedong and his disciples saw as progressive in secular Western history. With such an unintegrated mixture as a possible heritage, the Chinese people have little to feel certain about. The idea of simply training better leaders to master the Chinese heritage seems totally inadequate for what China needs to do. It cannot make up for institutions that have been shown to be no longer functional.

What about those who sought other models to help reinterpret the Confucian state? The hope that ideas from the world outside would strengthen core Chinese values with modern machines, technologies and methods, and that the rejuvenated elites arising from that transformation would dedicate themselves to radical reforms, still has appeal. Many questions, however, remain: why did their predecessors who embraced such a course fail? Why did the earlier reforms not prevent revolution and the overthrow of the old ruling classes? Those who had created the republic in 1911 seemed merely to have replaced one lot of rulers with another. They had not been equipped to deal with modernity, but were so divided from the start that anarchy seemed to have been unavoidable. What is to be learnt from that experience today?

The failures had led to a more pluralistic generation, most of whom were the products of progressive modern schools. They were exposed early to scientific and business skills and wanted the country to be fully sovereign and independent. Unfortunately, they were no less divided. Today, even more pluralistic educated groups may be found. There are larger numbers of them and they are better-prepared to explore new ideas and challenge the new orthodoxy than any previous generation. They are also no less determined to protect their country's interests. The question is, how are they to overcome the extensive corruption and the lack of a binding ideal that together threaten their unity?

Following the bold turnaround by Deng Xiaoping, this generation is disillusioned with Maoist shibboleths and have taken to wide-ranging economic reforms with determination. The conversion of these groups to a new faith in incremental development, something their predecessors had rejected, provides hope for future stability. They have accepted the ambiguities of a socialism adapting to the demands of a market economy. They are learning the values of new professional classes, and are increasingly aware of the need for new laws and institutions for a civic society. But they still have such a big country to modernise and it is clear from past experience that models good for others may not work for China. They are convinced now, as Deng

Xiaoping advised, that they have to feel for stones when crossing the river. It must be a relief to know that, after a century and a half, they seem to be better agreed which is the river they have to cross.

Two things are clear. Each of the elites of the past century and a half has had to meet different challenges and each has learnt lessons from earlier generations. What are the challenges for the coming decades? And what lessons are specially relevant?

The major challenges concern the changing shape of what countries of the dominant West regard as modern today. Where the economy is concerned, what is new for the present elites is a more dynamic global economy on which China must depend if it is to go on growing. This provides them with a hopeful agenda. Although belatedly, investments are being channelled into productive sectors in a systematic way. Non-performers are being replaced. Financial institutions are facing drastic reforms. But the pace is measured, sometimes one of fits and starts, and the question being asked again is whether there is now too much caution. It is well-known how Deng Xiaoping's "southern tour" in 1992 drove the economy forward at breathtaking speed. But the old charismatic approach to dramatic action has its dangers and may not suit the country now. The leaders today need to combine a new professionalism with administrative skills and financial and legal institutions that will ensure continuous and dependable improvement, something the country has never had.

Also new is the more unstable post-Cold War world order that is dominated by a powerful United States. This subject has increasingly engaged the attention of China's elites because they are conscious how ambivalent their predecessors had been about the role of the US in China's affairs. But the present ambivalence is more unpredictable than in the past because China is no longer weak and helpless and deserving of American sympathy. The

Chinese now dismiss the idea of an American love-hate relationship with China. They see it as a patronising one whereby the United States loves China when it is poor and wretched and ready to conform to US norms, but hates it when China is strong and wishes to act in its own interests and go its own way. A realistic relationship for the 21st century would be one in which there is mutual respect — not because the Chinese now know how to behave like Americans, but because they are accepted as people who really want a peaceful environment for their country's development. In order to achieve that, China would have to go on assuring its neighbours that it needs peace in the region as much as everyone else.

More dangerous are the persistent calls for self-determination by those who are hostile to China's undemocratic and empire-based state. This is a new threat to the national unity which several generations have laboriously worked for throughout the last century. The fear of disunity is deeply-rooted in China' history. In the last thousand years, the Chinese can only claim to have ruled their own country for 280 of those years. Two other periods saw China unified only through Mongol and Manchu conquests. In this context, the Japanese invasion of the 1930s was a very recent nightmare.

How is that fear to be faced? The question of sovereignty was one of the first principles that China had learnt from its encounters with the West. The first and second generations of leaders suffered when that sovereignty was lost, when foreign powers through their officials, traders and missionaries could influence how China should be run and, in some areas, actually direct its administration. While China's dismemberment was finally halted, the task of restoring control over lost territories remained at the top of China's agenda. No leader in China can afford to let any land go. Hence the Taiwan problem today. The challenge is how the new leaders today can protect national unity without resorting to arms, how they can persuade the world that China's rights are truly inviolable and applying the principle of self-determination to parts of China would be infinitely destabilising.

What are the lessons they have learnt from earlier generations? The most important ones concern the means by which they remain united and their ability to inspire a society that has become more pluralist.

The first lesson is vital. Ever since the fall of the Qing dynasty, new elites have been fragmented by fierce political rivalry. By the 1930s, there were only three major groups: the Nationalists, the Communists and the various liberal democrats in between. After 1949, when the communists won their victory on the mainland, it did not take long before serious disagreements brought divisions between those who sided with Mao Zedong and those who did not. That division led to the disastrous Cultural Revolution. The purges demoralised the country and, despite the success of many economic reforms, systemic resistance to these reforms remained. And now that the post Cold War world has brought fresh uncertainties and introduced new criteria of international conformity, the ability to preserve solidarity among themselves has become an important concern.

The second lesson is to recognise that a more open China has become increasingly pluralist and there must be accommodation for new and younger talent to be co-opted into their ranks. This is a major challenge when new norms continue to be determined externally, international norms that seem always to be just beyond China's reach. To meet such a challenge requires confidence and a sense of security which the elites do not now have. When China was too weak in the past to resist external pressures, its leaders had tried to meet these standards by impatiently, and sometimes irrationally, trying to outperform other countries and leapfrog stages of development. When that proved disastrous, the lesson learnt was that the country needed stability to work out for itself the rate of modernisation that would give it the best chance to make real and continuous progress.

Helping China achieve this goal has so far been accepted as being in the global interest. The Chinese elites themselves seem to have agreed that letting markets and economic laws guide the country's development is the way to go. But they fear that, unlike the years when it was China that wanted the quickest possible transformation through revolution, today it is the West that has become impatient for a faster rate of change and is pressing China to conform to new rules like democracy and human rights at the expense of their hard-won stability. There is now in China a combination of political conservatism accompanied by rising economic power that the country has not experienced since the beginning of the 18th century. The trading powers at that time had found this an obstacle to their interests. Eventually, the British led the way to force an opening, one that diminished China's sovereignty and, in the eyes of Chinese elites, brought about the calamities that dogged the country thereafter.

Is this a past that most Chinese are prepared to forget? Known to be pragmatic, rational and realistic, would they not prefer simply to take note and get on with their future? Questions like these highlight the fact that the bulk of the Chinese people have only just begun to enjoy and appreciate the benefits of the modernity that they have long wanted. Their leaders have not always deserved their trust, but they know that more ordinary people now are able to rise and join the ranks of the new ruling classes than ever before. The very pluralism of the elite groups today, however amorphous some of them may still be, marks a stage of modernity which the Chinese can build on. The economic reforms of the past two decades have been hopeful years, and a large number of

Chinese have enjoyed a prosperity they have not seen for 200 years.

I said at the beginning that China has been trying to join the modern world for 140 years. It has been a long and arduous road. The Chinese seemed always to be travelling either too slowly or too fast. With this generation, it would seem that its leaders have found a momentum the country can keep up with. Even if the pace may seem slow to some, the solution is not for China to speed up at the behest of outside powers, but find its own rhythm for the long haul. There is still an enormous task ahead. For lasting peace which every country in the region wants, coping with China calls for wisdom and patience from all concerned. The Chinese people have come such a long way this past century. If ever they needed some friendly help, it is now.

The Chinese Revolution and the Overseas Chinese[*]

It does seem timely to reflect on the impact of the Chinese re-volution on the *huaqiao* (Overseas Chinese). By overseas Chinese, I refer to those Chinese not living in territories traditionally regarded as part of China, that is, not of the People's Republic of China (hereafter the PRC), Taiwan, and the territories of Hong Kong and Macau. For example, Hong Kong and Taiwan Chinese are not overseas Chinese although they lived for a while under foreign jurisdiction.

Last year was the 50th Anniversary of the establishment of the PRC in 1949. For most Chinese living outside China at the time, this would have been their second or third experience of Chinese revolution. Many of the older *huaqiao* had been through the excitement of the 1911 republican revolution when the Qing dynasty was overthrown. Many others would remember the struggle to implement Sun Yat-sen's revolution against various warlords, and the founding of the Guomindang's nationalist

---

*This was a lecture given at Stanford University on 28 March 2000. It was part of a series of lectures organised to commemorate the 50th Anniversary of the People's Republic of China.

government in Nanjing in 1928. And many more would have been active in the civil war and the patriotic task of saving China from the Japanese, a series of most memorable events which ended in communist victory. Thus the Chinese abroad were no strangers to revolution in China. It may seem to have been a series of different revolutions but, to most of them, it was one continuing revolution striving to bring China into the modern world. What is important to stress is that these Chinese had always been divided by that revolutionary cause, by the different definitions and perceptions of revolution and by the leaders and the parties that claimed to represent it. In addition, some of these overseas Chinese were further divided by the policies of host governments outside China which were increasingly suspicious of the Chinese living in their territories and who engaged actively in the politics of China.

Are these experiences of the overseas Chinese different from those of other diasporic peoples? One should note that revolution is really a very modern phenomenon; thus the the link between diaspora and revolution could only have happened in recent history. Among Europeans who had left their homelands to go overseas, some also saw revolutions in their respective countries, notably the French, the German and the Young Italy revolutions. But, before the 20th century, there was little evidence of direct involvement in revolutions by those residing abroad: a few restorationist Frenchmen and some risorgimento Italians. It was not until this century that the politics of the diaspora became significant. Most dramatically, there were the Zionist movement for the return to Palestine of European Jewry and the overseas Irish support for independence from Great Britain, but also, there were the anti-communist politics of some Russians after 1917, of German sympathisers of Hitler, and then, after World War II, among anti-Soviet Czechs and Poles, the anti-Russian Baltic peoples and some anti-Yugoslavia Croats. Closer to China, there were diasporic Arabs, Kurds and Iranians who felt that their peoples had suffered unjust humiliation at the hands of the West, or at those of the Turkish and Israeli governments. Others in the diaspora were politically engaged because they had been displaced by dictatorial regimes at home, regimes which they desperately wanted to overthrow. We know how active these diasporas have been. But most of these examples became important only after the end of the Second World War.

Some other overseas Asian have had experiences more comparable to those of the Chinese, for example, the Indians in former European colonial territories, the Japanese in North America and, more recently, the Vietnamese in the United States and Australia. This is not the place to make detailed comparisons. I mention them only to remind us that similar links between diasporas and revolutionary changes at home can be found. The major differences, however, lie in that China alone has had an ongoing revolution for the greater part of the century, one that was accompanied by civil wars and foreign invasion, and that its *huaqiao* had been involved with them all from the start. In addition, China was the largest country to accept communism during the Cold War and it is still demonised by large numbers of anti-communists among whom the overseas Chinese still have to live. These circumstances gave the relationship between the Chinese revolution and the *huaqiao* some exceptional features. In this lecture, I propose to outline some of the most important of those features during the past half century.

I have been using the word *huaqiao*, usually translated as Overseas Chinese and meaning sojourners, that is, those Chinese who are temporarily living abroad and who intend to return to China. This is deliberate, for it is among them that the Chinese revolution has meant the most, as seen in the famous saying attributed to Sun Yat-sen, "the *huaqiao* is the mother of re-volution". The term came into common use at the beginning of this century and has carried political connotations ever since, especially when linked with patriotism, as in *aiguo huaqiao*. But, strictly speaking, despite its common usage, not all Chinese outside China considered themselves *huaqiao* even before the Pacific War. For example, Chinese who became subjects of the Siamese king, many Catholic Chinese in the Philippines, and some of those who became British, Dutch or French subjects in their respective colonies. Since the 1950s, the numbers of such Chinese have grown, especially among those in Southeast Asia who have found it necessary to distance themselves from the term *huaqiao* as one that is both inaccurate and outdated. Instead, words like *huaren* and *huayi* have been substituted for it. These reflect recent political and social changes in the region. If *huaqiao* are sojourning Chinese, *huaren* would be "nationalised" or ethnic Chinese, and *huayi* those "descendants of Chinese" who consider themselves politically integrated with their adopted countries if not culturally assimilated as well. There is some argument about how many generations must transpire before one may be called a *huayi*, but today it really represents the attitudes of those who, while being proud of being of Chinese origin, do not see themselves primarily as Chinese. Of the three terms, the first is clear and the third is self-defined. The second (*huaren*), however, remains difficult to pin down and can still be a source of misunderstanding. The greatest difficulty lies in the fact that the literal meaning of the word in English is "Chinese" while usage has made it apply to ethnic Chinese minorities who are citizens or nationals of non-Chinese countries. It is commonly used together with *haiwai*, thus *haiwai huaren*, which confusingly, actually translates as "overseas Chinese". And it does not help when many writers make no distinction whatsoever and still use "overseas Chinese" to cover every one outside China who is identifiably Chinese, which may smack of racism.

I have dwelt on the three terms here because their distinctive use may be seen as a product of the impact of the Chinese revolution and, certainly in Southeast Asia, is the result of the region's international politics pertaining to the PRC during the last 50 years. These distinctions are less understood in North America, but I suggest that they might eventually be useful there as well. For my purposes, I shall use shorthand references for the three in this lecture, as follows: sojourners for *huaqiao*, ethnic Chinese for *huaren*, and local nationals for *huayi*. By doing this, I make two points immediately. Firstly, there were already internal divisions within overseas Chinese communities dating from the first half of the century which determined their different responses to China politics during the second half. Secondly, in their varied responses to the Chinese revolution, the Chinese in Southeast Asia were, and still are, significantly different from those in North America. These two points provide a general background to the impact of the revolution as represented by the 1949 victory of the Chinese Communist Party on the China mainland.

To speak of the impact since 1949, we need to ask what numbers of overseas Chinese were involved. There has been no accurate count of the number of Chinese outside the PRC, Hong Kong-Macau and Taiwan when the PRC was founded. Good estimates would place the total in 1950 somewhere between eight and nine million around the world, of which some 90 per cent were resident in Southeast Asia. Today, the figure for *haiwai huaren* (the ethnic Chinese overseas), or the preferred term in the PRC, the *huaqiao-huaren* (the sojourners plus the ethnic Chinese), is not much more accurate. Most estimates suggest that the figure should be about 22–25 million, with about 80 per cent living in Southeast Asia and the bulk of the remainder in the English-speaking world of North America and Australasia. During the past 50 years, the number of Chinese overseas has nearly trebled but, because of the rate of integration and assimilation in some areas, not all those with part-Chinese blood can be described as Chinese, and many would reject such an identification. On the other hand, given changing conditions, for example, a stronger and more prosperous China or a local national leadership that is more sympathetic towards the PRC, those citizens of Chinese descent have been known to reidentify as Chinese, even though only for specific purposes. This does not help us determine accurate figures, and we have to be content with gross estimates.

For our purposes, however, the total figure is not important. We are primarily concerned with those sojourners and ethnic Chinese distributed all over the world who have looked to China for their needs and who could clearly be called *aiguo huaqiao* in 1949. From China's point of view, all overseas Chinese would qualify, but my own estimate would be that, at the end of the Pacific War, following the defeat of Japan and the elevation of China to membership of the United Nations Security Council, all the sojourners and the majority of all others would be prepared to be described as patriotic (*aiguo*). This did not mean that they would return to serve their country. Most would continue to live abroad and be ready to support their families and countrymen to the best of their ability. But the communist victory in 1949 did dampen the enthusiasm of those who had long been nationalistic and were wary of the PRC's alien commitments to the internationalist Marxist bloc. Guomindang followers, in particular, remained hostile to the PRC. Among younger Chinese, however, most were proud of a strong and united China and many were genuinely sympathetic with the cause of revolution. Of course, there were also those who were simply so disgusted with the corrupt regime in Nanjing that had moved to Taiwan that they embraced the new Beijing government.

There are no reliable figures as to how the overseas Chinese divided on this subject. What became obvious quite early on was that the divisions were influenced by the political leanings of the countries in which they were resident. In Southeast Asia, the end of colonial rule produced a totally new environment for the overseas Chinese there. There were now independent governments newly embarked on their nation-building programs. Thus, in countries which recognised Beijing, most Chinese would look to the PRC and, where the governments withheld recognition, there was the political space to support the government in Taipei. In this way, local Chinese commitment to the power politics in China was subject to the policies of the new regimes under which they had to live. The prime concern of most overseas Chinese was pride in a China that was respected by foreign states, respect that could translate into respect for them as ethnic Chinese and make the majority peoples in these states refrain from discrimination against them. They did not bargain for the global ideological division which local governments could use as a weapon to discriminate against them in other ways. This was particularly true of countries where the Chinese formed a small minority. For example, Sukarno's Indonesia leaned towards the PRC and the PRC embassy officials protected the Chinese who looked to them for help, while the Philippines followed the United States in recognising the Guomindang government in Taiwan and could, if they wished, punish local Chinese who were thought to be sympathetic to Beijing. These examples explain why, in the 1950s, the majority of the Chinese in Indonesia turned towards the PRC and the majority of those in the Philippines backed Taiwan.

A position similar to that in the Philippines could also be found in North America, especially in the United States, but for perhaps somewhat different reasons. In the 1950s and 1960s, the Chinese there were not under pressure to naturalise and they remained Chinese nationals far longer than in Southeast Asia. U.S. society as a whole was greatly hostile towards revolutionary ideology, and communism in particular. The Cold War was a sharp divide and there was little room for neutrality or ambiguity, especially if most Chinese were not even American citizens. Of course, this did not stop some patriotic sojourners from working on behalf of the new regime in Beijing in educational bodies, international institutions and in the media. But they received little help from the larger overseas Chinese community who tended to sympathise with U.S. policies. The fact that the Republic of China was represented in the United Nations in New York for more than twenty years was enough to ensure majority support. Over time, dismay over Chiang Kai-shek's dictatorial ways towards the Taiwanese, and some progressive and romantic representations of the revolution in China, did lead to changes in attitudes among the younger generation, but the overseas Chinese response had to be muted until other young Americans began to change their views about the PRC. The best example would be that of the Cultural Revolution of the late 1960s which evoked sympathy among the rebellious young for a few years. This played a part in arousing the activism of younger Chinese in the vigorous Diaoyutai movement against Japanese claims on tiny islands in the East China Sea. The movement provided a focus for patriotic feelings under conditions which deterred Chinese from openly and directly identifying with the

PRC and opposing the government in Taiwan. It also marked a significant change of national mood on the eve of a major shift in U.S. policy towards the PRC.

In short, for the first 20 years, Guomindang officials in North America were effective in claiming that it was the ROC that represented the Chinese revolution and the PRC was a betrayal and an aberration in allowing China to be subordinated to an alien Soviet revolution. Ultimately, as U.S. national interests led to new China policies, other views surfaced to counter that Guomindang claim. Increasingly, the view that the Guomindang had become reactionary and anti-revolutionary became more acceptable. This was reflected not only in the writings of the sojourners themselves, but more so in the national and ethnic Chinese media. Perspectives began to change towards the revolution itself, so much so that the destructive excesses of the Cultural Revolution were played down as the U.S. government moved towards the diplomatic recognition of the PRC. Instead, by the early 1970s, the contradictory sentiments aroused in the U.S. included, on the one hand, a mixture of admiration and disgust for the actions of revolutionary youth and, on the other, a readiness to welcome young Chinese to study in America, accompanied by a new missionary zeal to bring enlightenment to the spiritually impoverished in China. The situation changed again in the 1980s and I shall come back to that. Let me now turn to Southeast Asia during the first half of the period since 1949.

The situation in Southeast Asia was quite different. Of the current ten countries (East Timor is likely to be the eleventh, but is a special case whose story need not detain us), three can separated from the other seven. I refer the two states that had been British Malaya (that is, Malaysia and Singapore today) and the special case of Indonesia. These deserve fuller treatment here. This is not the place to go into how the Chinese in each of the other seven countries responded to China. Let me give a brief outline to emphasise some common points. These latter communities are relatively small, between one and five per cent of the total population of each country. There was considerable variety among different groups of Chinese in each of their responses to the Chinese revolution. In these countries, the majority were engaged in businesses large and small. For them, there were few options other than to hide their often ambiguous feelings about China. The tendency was for the majority in each Chinese community to accept the official China policies which their respective governments espoused. That meant, to rejoice when these were pro-China and to keep their heads down when these were hostile. On the whole, as businessmen, they exercised great care not to offend their respective governments, while trying not to miss any opportunity to trade with Chinese agencies (whether based in the PRC or in Taiwan, but best if they operated out of Hong Kong). If they resided in capitalist countries, they knew there would be no sympathy for communist ideas. If they lived in communist or socialist societies, there was clearly no room for most of their kinds of businesses.

Let me now turn to the remaining three countries in the region. In some ways, Indonesia resembled the other seven: the Chinese population was small, about 3 per cent of the total, and the majority had little choice but to submit to national government policies towards the PRC and Taiwan. But there were exceptional conditions. Firstly, the bulk of the Chinese were visibly better off in the urban centres throughout the country. Secondly, President Sukarno was clearly on the side of the PRC from 1950 to 1965, while his successor President

Suharto radically changed the government's position to one of hostility and suspicion for the next 25 years. That shift marked the Chinese revolution's direct impact on Chinese lives and livelihood in the country. Clearly the impact was neither consistent nor predictable. In a matter of weeks in 1965, a violent local revolution had taken place or, in the eyes of some, there had been a Communist Chinese plot that was followed by a murderous reaction that turned the world upside down for most Chinese. The results were not all negative. Many of those who had suffered during Sukarno's 15 years did very well because of the change and became wealthy beneficiaries of Suharto's 32 years.

There is evidence that many younger Chinese in the 1950s did admire the ideals of the Chinese revolution. Some became ardent supporters of the Indonesian Communist Party while others chose to return to China to work for the new China. However, it is not clear how accurate the figures were of those who were considered to be Chinese citizens in the mid-1950s. About one million out of an estimated two and a half million represented those who identified with revolution. Certainly, we know most of them had no choice because they did not qualify as Indonesian citizens. During the 1960s, when choice became possible, the majority applied to be Indonesians. Thereafter, it would have been difficult to find amongst them any who supported the excesses of the Cultural Revolution in the PRC. By force of circumstances, most Chinese Indonesians were driven to accept business careers and capitalist goals because many avenues of normal employment, for example, in the civil service, were denied to them. Their violent swing from a willingness to go along with communist revolution in China to a grim commitment to market economy ways marked the extreme conditions under which most ethnic

Chinese had to adapt their lives. These wrenching experiences have come to distinguish such Chinese from their counterparts elsewhere.

This brings me to the former British territories that have now become the two states of Malaysia and Singapore. There were altogether 15 such territories at the end of the Second World War: three colonies which were directly under British rule, four sultanates which the British administered on behalf of the Malay rulers, six others of which they were officially only protectors, and two which received special protection from the British, that is, the Brooke family's heritage of Sarawak and the North Borneo Company's territory now known as Sabah. I stress the fragmentary characteristics of the two countries now called Malaysia and Singapore because these multiple origins explain the different degrees of control the British had over the various Chinese communities in each of these states and territories, and also why the differences allowed these communities more freedom to organise themselves than was possible elsewhere in Southeast Asia.

It was not only until 1947, on the eve of a communist insurgency on the Malay peninsula and only two years before the communist victory in China, that 11 of the territories on the Malay peninsula came together, to be called the Federation of Malaya. At this point, about two and a half million or some 38.4 per cent of the Federation's population were Chinese, while in Singapore, the 730,000 Chinese constituted about 77 per cent of the total population there. The preponderance of Chinese in Singapore was the main reason why Singapore was left out and remained a British colony. From the Malay point of view, the fact that the Chinese in four of the eleven states already averaged over 50 per cent of each state's total population, and that Chinese constituted over 40 per cent of two other states, made future nation-building a serious problem. Thus the Malay leaders, supported by the British, would rather not have Singapore as part of the federation.**

Leaving out the island of Singapore was a decision that is very relevant to our story. Had Singapore been included, the Chinese population would have outnumbered the native Malay peoples, something the Malay sultans and aristocracy and the new nationalist leaders simply could not accept. They had experienced the rise of Chinese nationalism in response to revolution in China and, during the 1920s and 1930s, saw this nationalism unite most Chinese against the Japanese. After the Pacific War, this had turned into a liberation war against British imperialism and the communist leadership of that war could have placed the Chinese in a dominant position in an independent Malaya. The Malay leaders could not allow this and worked closely with the departing British to prevent this from happening. Thus,

---

**The following are the most significant figures for the Chinese population in various parts of British Malaya in 1947:

1. 38.4% Chinese, that is, a total of 1,885,000 (Federation of Malaya). In comparison, 49.2% were Malays (a total of 2,428,000 out of a total population of 4,908,000.

2. In Singapore, the figures were 77% Chinese, totalling 729,473 as compared with 12% Malays, totalling 113,803.

3. For the purpose of comparison, figures for other Malay states where the Chinese are present in sizable numbers are as follows:

Penang	55.4%
Selangor	51%
Johore	48.1%
Perak	46.6%
Malacca and Negri Sembilan both had over	40%

the Chinese revolution was the underlying factor why great care was taken to align with anti-communist forces in post-colonial Malaya and exclude local Chinese from key positions in the government and the military.

Herein lies one of the most important manifestations in Southeast Asia of China's revolution — the formation of revolutionary parties largely inspired by a Marxist-Leninist anti-imperialism that began in Europe and spread east and spawning communist parties among the overseas Chinese. Where the Chinese were few in number, there was among them no sizable working class nor a middle-class intelligentsia. Only in the British and Dutch territories were there the numbers of overseas Chinese to produce a potentially revolutionary base, and only in British Malaya and northern Borneo were there Chinese groups that could be described as acting as a radical proletariat. Not surprisingly, it was among these Chinese that the potential for armed revolution was found.

There are now several major studies of the origins of the Communist Party of Malaya (the CPM). Clearly, despite the success of British efforts at breaking up the early cells, it was the left-wing idealists driven out of China by civil war during the years 1928–1937 who laid the foundations of the Party, and it was their disciples who sustained it during the war against the Japanese in Malaya. That fact both inspired the notion of revolution and bedevilled it after the Malayan Emergency was declared in 1948. It created the image of the CPM as an import from China, which the Party never succeeded in removing, no matter how hard its leaders like Chin Peng (Chen Ping) and his few Malay and Indian colleagues tried. The fact that the PRC and all socialist countries, for ideological reasons, gave the Party moral and material support, and Britain, the U.S. and their allies, including Taiwan, gave this support prominence in their propaganda against communism, helped to isolate and prevent any drive to revolution among the general population.

Thus, while it can be said that the Chinese revolution inspired a similar revolution in Malaya, it also contributed to its ultimate defeat. Given that the Chinese numbers were large, would the outcome have been different if external factors had not played so strong a part in the revolution? Perhaps the 38.4 per cent Chinese population would have ended eventually with less than 38.4 per cent power and more than 38.4 per cent wealth even if the Chinese revolution had not had any influence in Malaya. I shall not speculate on that here. As for other aspects of the Chinese revolution and how they impacted on the region, I shall come to that in the final section of this lecture.

Let me return to the expectation in the 1950s that Singapore should have been part of a single country called Malaya. That possibility had raised hopes among some that revolution was an anti-colonial reality the region had to accept. It was thought that the large number of Chinese in Singapore would allow them to link their fate with that of revolution in China if they wished to; it certainly helped them claim the political right to determine the kind of country they would want to live in. These hopes coloured thinking about how an independent Malaya should one day include Singapore. Under the glaring light of Indonesia's Confrontation policy, the British made new territorial arrangements to include Sarawak and Sabah that enabled Singapore to join the larger federation called Malaysia, and the merger was achieved in 1963. It did not last long. After more than a year of turmoil in which ethnic Chinese rights were in dispute and race riots left hundreds killed, Singapore was ejected in August, 1965.

This was a fateful decision. What part did the Chinese revolution play in the drama that unfolded? The PRC had supported President Sukarno in his opposition to the formation of

Malaysia. Weeks after the ejection of Singapore, the Indonesian military annihilated the Indonesian Communist Party and greatly strengthened anti-communist and anti-Chinese forces in the region. Most Chinese who had sympathised with revolution in China were removed from the political arena. For those who survived, there was little room for neutrality or ambiguity. Ethnic Chinese confronted the great divide as revolution in Vietnam backed by the Soviet Union and the PRC broke the region effectively into two. Three-quarters of the Chinese in Southeast Asia were located in the anti-revolutionary half that eventually became, in 1967, members of the Association of Southeast Asian Nations (ASEAN). Many Chinese began to vote with their feet to leave the region, not to go to China but to migrant nations in North America and Australasia and any country that would welcome the better educated among them. By then, the PRC was no longer an attraction. Following the failures of the Great Leap Forward, the Maoist economics that led to national famines, and the start of the Cultural Revolution early in 1966, ethnic Chinese had fewer options. They could turn further outwards away from China and the region wherever they could, or make their peace with the new nation-building countries where they had settled down. In less than twenty years after revolutionary victory in China, the appeal of revolution was dead for most ethnic Chinese in Southeast Asia.

No one in 1965 could have predicted the outcome of Singapore's independence. The complex circumstances that led to the formation of first Malaya and then Malaysia included the long shadow of the Chinese revolution. But the tide turned in the mid-1960s. Even as the Soviets and the PRC backed the Vietnamese to win their war against the U.S. and its allies, the Chinese revolution was losing the hearts and minds of the Chinese overseas in Southeast Asia. Although the impact of revolution on the Chinese communities had left a deep impression, a new chapter had begun following the deep split within the communist bloc between its largest powers, Russia and China. Early in the 1970s, spectacular diplomatic initiatives led to the PRC's admission into the United Nations at the expense of Taiwan. These led to extensive changes in policies towards China and cleared the way for a different face of revolution to be painted.

Perhaps the most significant of all changes was the exposure of the self-destructive revolution in the PRC itself. Chairman Mao's deadly efforts to remake the Chinese Communist Party opened the eyes of Chinese both inside and outside China. The absurdities of revolutionary rhetoric were so extreme that, by the end of the 1970s, with the return of Deng Xiaoping, the word revolution had totally lost its appeal. The most remarkable turnaround came when most Chinese overseas responded with undisguised relief and pleasure when the word revolution left the present and became a memory and an historical concept.

Have these ethnic Chinese been inconsistent, naive, hypocritical, filled with romance and wishful thinking about the Chinese revolution? Or did they only appear so? We do not have enough detailed studies of their varied responses to answer such questions as yet. After all, even the way the Chinese in China embraced revolution and then set it aside has not been fully understood. All I can offer here are some preliminary thoughts about how this vast subject might be approached.

I believe we will always be perplexed unless we start with the rise of nationalist revolution under the aegis of the movements which supported men like Sun Yat-sen. These had ranged from popular associations with anti-Manchu credentials to merchant groups who longed for China to play its rightful role in the world, and to new intelligentsia educated outside the country who admired the revolutions that had modernised the powerful nations of the West. The delight of Sun Yat-sen in 1897 when he saw that, to the world outside China, he was not merely a *pan-nie* (rebel), but *kakumeisha*, or *gemingzhe* (revolutionary) is well-known. That was recognition and legitimation in the eyes of the world, the new image which raised his actions to a higher plane. He never looked back. The word *geming*, revolution, stayed with him until his dying day, and is still the word associated with him among those who remember him today, whether in the PRC, Hong Kong and Taiwan, or among the Chinese overseas.

In short, *geming* had been a heritage of modern China. Its transformation from nationalist revolution to social and economic, and then communist, revolution was far less important among most Chinese than the fact that it stood for a new China, one that would be restored to wealth and power by heroic leaders. The means needed to achieve that desired end would vary and those who found the correct path to bring such a revolution to China deserved great respect. The *huaqiao* or sojourner Chinese believed this no less fervently than those at home. The earliest supporters of Sun Yat-sen in Hawaii, Yokohama and Kobe, San Francisco, or Vancouver, had offered financial support. Similarly, with those in Singapore, Penang, Ipoh, Kuala Lumpur, Saigon, or Hanoi, but amongst these were many who returned to fight for revolution and some who died. The connection became legendary. The fact that they had contributed to the revolution's beginnings from outside the country rarely failed to tug at the hearts of these overseas Chinese if not also their purse-strings for decades to come. To these people far away from home, with mixed feelings of relief and guilt, this was the least they could have done.

All this continued despite the fact that the revolution did not do well for half a century. Sun Yat-sen's presidency in 1912 was the shortest on record. Warlords and local banditry terrorised the country for the next decade and a half. Sun Yat-sen's domestic followers who went among the sojourners began to divide into nationalists, communists, anarchists, westernised liberals and democrats. Still, they were welcome as long as they stood for different roads towards the same goal of the revolution — a modern China. Disappointments followed throughout the 1920s and 1930s, but the overseas Chinese were galvanised by fresh dangers when the Japanese invaded China. Thus, the patriotic war, the salvation efforts, the boycotts of Japanese goods, the volunteers to fight on Chinese soil were all part and parcel of the revolution that had long been denied them. No wonder the excitement when the end of the Pacific War was followed by the ultimate victory of Mao Zedong's armies in the name of what was then considered by many to be the most genuine revolution of them all.

Were the overseas Chinese much interested in the content of the Chinese revolution? There is early evidence of debate among supporters of Kang Youwei, or the pro-emperor constitutionalists, and those of Sun Yat-sen, or the pro-republic nationalists, before 1911. When the republic was established and needed substance, the newspapers read by the sojourners distinguished between selfish militarists and idealistic patriots who carried the nationalist flag. For twenty years after 1928, most sojourners looked to the Guomindang state as China's only chance for survival. They were saddened by a civil war between nationalists and communists they did not fully understand and did not really approve of, especially when it spread the contagion far and wide. The media available to these sojourners did explain the major thrusts of the ideological divide, and many took sides in fierce exchanges.

Among the larger communities of the sojourners where many modern schools were established, politicised teachers brought revolutionary ideas of every complexion to prepare the younger generation for the day when they would return to China, either to study or to work. Precisely how most sojourners placed themselves on China's political agenda is difficult to calculate. The evidence is that most sojourners cared and some were drawn to do battle for their version of revolution. But for the long haul, the struggle for livelihood engaged their energies far more, and in each community were increasing numbers who came to care less for China's politics as the party disputes seemed endless and even futile. By the end of World War II, sojourners and ethnic Chinese alike longed for peace and reconstruction of a battered country and a devastated economy. The growing disgust at corruption in high places and runaway inflation deterred many sojourners from returning to China. Already, a clear majority had determined that their future lay outside, even that they could help China more by being abroad than in China itself.

Were they more impressed with the focused goals of the communists revolution after 1949? Some radical youth among the Chinese overseas cheered the removal of the corrupt politicians and bureaucrats of the previous regime, the violent land reforms in the countryside, and the dismantling of the old social structures. Others also welcomed the replacement of ancient traditions by what they thought was a modern and progressive outlook. Some went so far as to return to China in the belief that they could help in China's reconstruction. In any case, for most Chinese overseas, whatever their age and persuasion, they were conscious of living outside the country. The specifics were not relevant. It was not for them to determine what China really needed. What certainly evoked applause amidst surprise was Mao Zedong's spectacular military victory. The fact that this was followed by unification on the mainland, for the first time since 1911, had a strong impact among all of them. Chinese tradition itself encouraged the idea that success was the ultimate proof of truth and greatness. But there were also feelings of longing and hope: this time, these new leaders would give the people the peace and prosperity they had not had for more than a century. Beyond that, it is doubtful if many outside China cared what the new classics of Marx, Lenin, Stalin and Mao contained. There were appealing parts in the ideals they represented. These included the nationalist bits in Mao's speeches and some of the egalitarian rhetoric but, for a while, what attracted most admiration was the strategic thinking that led to his final victory and to a new dignity for China.

Sojourners who could be called patriotic (*aiguo*) *huaqiao* would love China anyway. Ethnic Chinese were largely involved in the sinews of competitive commerce and were normally shy of politics of any kind. Local nationals identified with what their own governments supported. There is little evidence that communist programs were in themselves important except to some of the students and proletariat among the Chinese in Malaya and Singapore. Elsewhere, the appeal was greater among the indigenous peoples, and a few idealistic young Chinese did join local communist movements. But the key was always the presence of China itself, the image of strength it projected, the respect it aroused and the authority it exuded. On the whole, sojourners could not have enough of that. Ethnic Chinese felt a deep pride to be Chinese and welcomed the help which that presence would give to their safety and their livelihood. As for local nationals, that is, Chinese with local citizenship, they had always longed for the day when their Chinese ancestry would be an asset and not a liability. Thus, with the return of Deng Xiaoping in 1978 and the substitution of economic reforms for social and political upheavals, there was a new beginning in which revolution was no longer the magic word. Finally, there was a new convergence between the PRC's major goals and the aspirations of the Chinese overseas which has been nothing short of marvellous.

The long Chinese revolution towards modernity has given most Chinese overseas great hope, but has also brought them much grief. What is their verdict today? They would first wonder if the revolution is finally over. Is the socialist market economy, and whatever comes after, the final stage of the revolution started by Sun Yat-sen? If it is, there would be relief accompanied by sadness that it has been such a bitter and painful road to get to where China is now. If, however, the present rejection of the word revolution is but a pause on a yet more tortuous road ahead, it would be unlikely that the Chinese outside would ever embrace yet another Chinese revolution again. It has been a long century and the Chinese have endured much in the name of revolution because they had high expectations of the leaders who espoused it. The world itself has changed, in other ways probably more revolutionised than China has ever been. The new generations, whether sojourners, ethnic Chinese or local nationals, can better judge what should lie ahead than any of their forbears could. These Chinese overseas have settled in their new homes round the world; the better educated and more skilled among them are increasingly international in outlook. In the decades to come, they are likely to see the Chinese revolution as history, part inspiring and glorious, part tragic and futile, a subject that can still evoke awe and tears, but they may well conclude that revolution in China has done its best and worst and they need to move on.

A Single Chinese Diaspora?*

I wish to begin by thanking Professor Reid and his colleagues for their efforts in establishing this new Centre for the study of the Chinese overseas. It had started modestly as a series of lectures to remember Jennifer Cushman, a friend whom we all miss dearly. That series led to the volume entitled *Sojourners and Settlers* which Tony Reid published a couple of years ago.[1] Not content with that, he set out to plan this Chinese Southern Diaspora Centre. He and his colleagues are convinced that the subject of the Chinese who migrated and settled southwards is deserving of serious study, and that the ANU is the right place to locate such

*This is a revised version of the inaugural lecture of the Centre for the Study of the Chinese Southern Diaspora, Australian National University, Canberra, February 1999. The lecture was given on 26th February, 1999 and an earlier text was published by the Centre as one of two essays in *Imagining the Chinese Diaspora: Two Australian Perspectives*. By Wang Gungwu and Annette Shun Wah. Canberra: Centre for the Study of the Chinese Southern Diaspora, Australian National University, 1999, pp. 1–17. The earlier version has been translated into Chinese by Zhao Hongying and published in *Huaqiao huaren lishi yanjiu* (Beijing), no. 3, September, 1999, pp. 1–14.

a centre. I agree. Australia does need to encourage teaching and research in this field and the ANU has excellent facilities to get this job done well. It is most gratifying to see it take off now. I am delighted that Tony invited me to give the Centre's inaugural lecture. I need hardly say that this is a Centre I want to be associated with. What I have to say this evening is but a small measure of congratulations to the team that made this Centre possible.

You are probably so used to the phrase Chinese Southern Diaspora by now that you may be surprised that I should want to reflect on the use of the term diaspora here. After all, I recently called the two volumes of essays which Wang Ling-chi and I edited, *The Chinese Diaspora*.[2] I had to do some heart-searching about that. I have long advocated that the Chinese overseas be studied in the context of their respective national environments, and taken out of a dominant China reference point. It is necessary that each Chinese community overseas be open to comparative study, both among themselves and together with other migrant communities. Our two volumes stressed settlement, as in the phrase *luodi shenggen*,[3] meaning growing roots where you land, and also differentiation among the communities in six continents. The 35 essays emphasise the great variety among Chinese who have found new homes in different parts of the world.

I still have some disquiet about the use of the term diaspora, not because, in English, it has until recently applied only to the Jews (see Oxford English Dictionary), nor because the word refers to exile (in Hebrew) or dispersion (in Greek), which are rather specific manifestations of the phenomenon of sojourning and migration.[4] Of course, it is misleading and politically sensitive for the Chinese to be compared to the Jews in the Muslim world of Southeast Asia, but if the reality makes the comparison appropriate, so be it.

My reservations come from the problems the Chinese encountered with the concept of sojourner (*huaqiao*) and the political use both China and hostile governments have made of that term. From China's point of view, *huaqiao* was a powerful name for a single body of overseas Chinese. It was openly used to bring about ethnic if not nationalist or racist binding of all Chinese at home and abroad. In the countries which have large Chinese minorities, that term had become a major source of the suspicion that the Chinese minorities could never feel loyalty towards their host nations. After some thirty years of debate, the term *huaqiao* now no longer includes those Chinese with foreign passports, and is being replaced by others like (*haiwai*) *huaren* and *huayi*, which disclaim formal China connections. The question which lingers in my mind is: will the word diaspora be used to revive the idea of a single body of Chinese, reminiscent of the old term, the *huaqiao*? Is this intended by those Chinese who favour its use? Once the term is widely used, would it be possible to keep it as a technical term in the social sciences, or will it acquire the emotive power that would actually change our views about the nature of the various Chinese communities overseas?

Tony Reid knows my reservations and has encouraged me to look back and reflect on how the Chinese abroad have been studied so far and how the approaches in the past have contributed to the present stage of evolution. This would also give me a chance to examine some of my own premises. My early interest in overseas Chinese history came from three major strands of scholarship. The first was that of the Chinese and Japanese scholars who gave the overseas Chinese a single identity as *huaqiao*, Chinese sojourners. This began with Chinese mandarins at the end of the 19th century, then came the reformers and revolutionaries and their Japanese supporters of the early 20th.[5] Finally the subject was taken up by scholars like Li Changfu, Liu Shimu, Wen Xiongfei and the team in Jinan University in Shanghai who founded, in the 1920s, the first major centre for the study of the *huaqiao*. They were followed by Chen Da, Zhang Liqian, Xu Yunqiao (Hsu Yun-ts'iao), and Yao Nan, the latter three helping to found the Nanyang Xuehui (The South Seas Society) in Singapore in 1940.[6]

The second strand was that of the colonial officials and the scholars they encouraged and commissioned to study the Chinese in the different territories of Southeast Asia. This was developed from their early trading experiences with the various kinds of Chinese which the Portuguese, Spanish, Dutch and English dealt with as they expanded their trading interests in Southeast Asia and the China coasts. Later, the Dutch, British and French adminis-trators studied their respective Chinese groups with particular care.[7] They saw the Chinese both as potential allies and as possible threats to their regimes. In the 20th century, Victor Purcell began writing seriously about them in the 1930s and, when he produced his comprehensive study for Southeast Asia in 1951, he emerged as the best example of this group's work.[8] The British Colonial Office after the war funded excellent scholars like Maurice Freedman and Tian Jukang, and their field research set new standards of anthropological enquiry.[9]

The third strand was the work of more recent field scholars, including sociologists and anthropologists who had wanted to study China but were forced to turn to the overseas Chinese when the communist victory in 1949 made it impossible for them to work in China itself. The leading figure in this strand was the American scholar Bill Skinner who worked on the Chinese in Thailand, while others worked on the distinct communities in Indonesia, Malaya, the Philippines and also Cambodia.[10] The China orienta-tion of the scholars in the latter two strands was obvious when Freedman and Skinner led them to come together to launch the very productive and significant London-Cornell project that studied

Hong Kong and Taiwan as the only Chinese societies that were accessible to non-Chinese scholars. The second and third strands inspired a new generation of scholars, including Southeast Asians of Chinese descent.[11]

It is significant that none of them used the term diaspora, and all of them treated the term *huaqiao*, that emphasised the oneness of the overseas Chinese identity, with reservations. Maurice Freedman, who was editor of the *Jewish Journal of Sociology*, and knew the Jewish connotations of diaspora best, did not consider the term appropriate for the Chinese. Instead, non-Chinese scholars favoured two distinct approaches: firstly, the study of varieties of *huaqiao* in different environments and the Chinese characteristics each of them retained and secondly, the study of the conditions under which the Chinese might assimilate and accept their place as citizens of the new nation-states of Southeast Asia.[12]

We all know that, early this century, the Chin se were compared with the Jews in Europe.[13] After Nazi persecution and the Holocaust, more recent scholars have been hesitant to use the comparison directly. The first person to raise the issue with me was not a student of the overseas Chinese, but of Indonesia. This was the late Harry Benda. His family were victims of the Holocaust in Czechoslovakia, he lived for many years in Dutch East Indies and he returned to study the new nation of Indonesia.[14] He suggested to me when we met in 1959 that the fate of the Chinese there could be similar to that of the Jews in Germany and I disagreed with him. In fact, as far as I know, he refrained from using the term diaspora in his writings. This was perhaps because he did see each Chinese community as seeking to develop its own distinctive identity away from the one that nationalist Chinese scholars and officials, and some local community leaders, had tried to impose on them. He knew that new political conditions in Southeast Asia during the 1950s were forcing the Chinese to reconsider what nationalism meant for them outside China.

I did not set out to study the Chinese overseas. My interest was always in Chinese history. This is partly because I started life as a Chinese sojourner, a *huaqiao*, someone temporarily resident abroad. If circumstances permitted it, such a person would look foremost to China. I was no exception. My father had come to the region to teach in high schools in Singapore, Kuala Lumpur and Malacca before becoming a principal of the first Chinese high school in Surabaya, where I was born. After he left Surabaya, he became assistant inspector of Chinese schools in Ipoh, in the state of Perak. This was a town with a Chinese majority, with the Malays in nearby suburban kampongs and most Indians housed by European-owned companies or government agencies. Among the Chinese, the tin miners in the Kinta valley were mostly Hakka, and the shopkeepers in the town mostly Cantonese. There was also a mixture of Hokkien, Teochiu and Hainanese, and smaller numbers who spoke other dialects. In short, it was a multi-communal town under Anglo-Malay administration, fairly typical of those in the four Federated Malay States of Malaya.

I was made aware very early that many of the sojourner families I grew up with thought in terms of returning to China one day. Others were ambivalent. They were happy to be out of China, to have a relatively secure living, and seemed content with a local polity that did not interfere much with their lives. Among the Chinese friends I made in the English school that I attended, however, I found many for whom China meant little. Their families had adapted fully to local living and typically spoke, read and wrote Malay and English better than they could any kind of Chinese. To them and to most of the teachers, my concern for the condition of China and for things Chinese was not readily comprehensible.

The events that highlighted the question of Chinese identity for me were the Japanese incursions into China that reached a climax in 1937 with a full-scale invasion. By that time, most Chinese were well accustomed to the rise of Chinese nationalist sentiment among the Chinese resident abroad. China politics had been brought to Overseas Chinese sojourners at the turn of the century.[15] It attracted their interest because of the anti-Chinese discriminatory acts around the world, the most virulent occurring in the migrant states of the Americas, Australasia and South Africa.[16] Such acts in Southeast Asia were less hurtful, on the whole, because the colonial powers, unlike the working classes of the European migrant states, found the Chinese useful to their trading and industrial enterprises.

Chinese nationalism spread quickly through the schools and newspapers that mushroomed in the 1910s and 1920s. In this atmosphere, *huaqiao* studies received overt political support in China. I became aware of this literature through my father and his teacher and journalist friends, but thought little of it. What was real was the propaganda conducted to arouse overseas Chinese to save China from the Japanese. After 1937, teams of people travelled around to raise funds for the war in China, to exhort all Chinese to buy Chinese manufactured goods and boycott everything Japanese.[17] A concerted effort was made to persuade overseas Chinese to think in terms of a single Chinese nation, something like what a single and united Chinese diaspora might imply. Success included collecting large donations sent to help the war effort and recruiting young Chinese workers and students to return to China to serve in the armed forces.[18]

During the Japanese occupation period, the sense of Chinese identity grew among everyone of Chinese descent. It was forced upon them, since they were seen as potential enemies. It did not matter if they cared for China, or were more loyal to local or colonial regimes. This background explains why many saw themselves simply as Chinese. It was natural that they should study the Chinese language and live as Chinese and, if they had the chance to do so, return to serve China. For myself, I prepared myself to return to China one day, and studied Chinese with my father with increasing interest and commitment.[19]

This did not cut me off from a rich variety of friendships. In study, in play and in the neighbourhood around my home, especially after the end of the war, I spent far more time with my Malay, Indian, Eurasian and non-Chinese speaking Chinese neighbours and schoolmates than with Chinese who thought like I did. The growing sense of being Malayan was something I understood and sympathised with, as it became clear that a new country would someday emerge from the colony-protectorate that the British had put together. That empire was coming to an end. The feeling of a local nationalism was growing among my friends.[20] I would like to have shared it with them, but I had a prior duty, and in 1947, I entered my father's old university in Nanjing.[21]

Dramatic political changes in China changed my life. The civil war was about to reach Nanjing, the university closed down, and this led me to rejoin my parents in Ipoh at the end of 1948.[22] When China became communist the next year, I was enrolled at the University of Malaya in Singapore and back among the kinds of friends I had made in school. Most of them were English-educated Chinese who had grown up in cities and towns with Chinese majorities.[23] It was easy for me to identify with them as Chinese, although it was clear that most of them had never been *huaqiao* sojourners like me. For them, they were home, and the projected nation of an independent Malaya was full of promise. For me, the turbulent Chinese nation had become increasingly an abstract entity dedicated to an ideology that seemed alien to the region. Through the prevailing anti-colonialism in Malaya and an Anglo-socialist perspective, I became reconciled to acquiring a new national identity. It was the first step to moving away from being a sojourner towards a conscious decision to settle outside of China. What I would become eventually was still uncertain, but learning to be a citizen of the Federation of Malaya was a beginning. Nevertheless, the commitment to know China remained: that is, to finish what I had started to do, to understand what could have gone wrong with that ancient civilisation, and what future it still had. Between sojourning and settling down in one place, I discovered that being Chinese was not a handicap but an anchor. Turning thus to the study of Chinese history seemed to be the most natural thing to do.

Thus, I set my mind to be a Chinese historian. Despite the pull of the politics of new nationhood in Malaya, I held to this course. But nation-building was a delicate matter, and new approaches towards history were required. I joined my colleagues to stimulate research on Malayan history, especially so that we might train a new generation of national historians among our students. For myself, I would contribute by studying the Malayan Chinese as they evolved from sojourners to citizens, as they learnt what it meant to be Malayans. I had given a series of radio talks in 1958 which were published as *A Short History of the Nanyang Chinese*.[24] My work on Chinese history had enabled me to relate the story from the beginning of Chinese relations with the region — the Nanhai trade, to the Cheng Ho naval expeditions and the defensive tributary system, and then to the coolie trade, the Nanyang merchant networks and the patriotic *huaqiao*. I read the local writings, the historical documents, and also the new scholarship on the changing Chinese communities with greater attention, notably the work of Western social scientists of the

1950s. At the same time, the most dramatic developments in the country included the steps taken in the years 1961 to 1965 to form a new Malaysian federation by joining together several former British territories with large Chinese communities.[25] This provided me with a focal point to embark on a comparative study of various Chinese communities trying to adapt to new political realities.

The Malaysia merger was accompanied by Indonesian Confrontation and ended as a failed experiment that threatened good relations between Chinese and Malays. 1965–1966 became a pivotal year for my research. The ejection of Singapore from Malaysia was a bitter blow. In the region, the Vietnam war had begun in earnest and the Sukarno regime ended with a terrifying bloodletting.[26] It was a turning-point for Southeast Asian development Even more dramatic was the unchaining of Mao Zedong and his effort to consolidate the revolution in China with a Proletarian Cultural Revolution. No one expected that this would eventually lead to the unravelling of Mao's vision in the midst of extensive anarchic conditions.

My interest in Chinese history was revived by the incredible stories reported about China. Was there method in Mao's madness? Was it necessary so that the revolution could escape from the deep-rooted Chinese past? Also, my work on Chinese history had gained attention, and I had to make a difficult choice. Should I stay and continue studying the Chinese in the region at a crucial point of change, or to return to my first love, the history of China as it was being reexamined and reinterpreted to meet the transformations on the mainland? In the end, it seemed to me that, at the ANU, I could hope to do both, to study China itself while remaining in the larger Southeast Asian neighbourhood. In Australia, I would never be far from at least the many groups of overseas Chinese close by.

I came to Canberra in 1968 and proceeded to indulge myself in all the books, pamphlets, journals, magazines, newspapers and miscellaneous documents that came out of the Cultural Revolution that had intensified in deadly earnest since 1966. This material was not available in Malaysia during the many years I worked in Kuala Lumpur. It took years before I felt I had caught up on Chinese affairs. Nevertheless, the first two articles I wrote at the ANU were "Chinese Politics in Malaya" and "Malaysia: Contending Elites".[27] I could now study both China and the Chinese communities outside. And because of that, the interplay between China's view of those communities and the view of themselves by the Chinese outside was never far from my mind. This interplay has guided my main writings till this day.

By seeking to connect both perspectives, I have not accepted China's view that China alone has the capacity to give the overseas Chinese what they need in order to remain Chinese. Chinese officials have always underestimated the resources the Chinese overseas have been able to muster to cultivate new kinds of Chineseness among themselves.[28] On the other hand, there has also been a sense of cultural inferiority that has often dogged those outside China. It seems to me that this has made them too modest about their achievements, whether in business, in education, or in technology. Their self-estimation has never been stable or well-judged, and they were wont to move from cultural cringe one moment to naive boastfulness the next.[29] There are many levels and dimensions in the subtle and uncertain relationships between China and its wandering peoples.

As for scholarly approach, I never tried to do what Maurice Freedman and Bill Skinner did systematically, which was to use what they learnt from the Chinese overseas to explain Chinese society itself.[30] Nor did I focus on the many past and present patterns of Chinese assimilation, nor agree with the studies that looked only at the new norms in Chinese responses to Southeast Asian nationalism. Instead, my work has tended to move between two wishful but ambiguous positions. One was China's wish to see all Chinese abroad as ultimately sojourners, as members of one extended Chinese family whose loyalty and patriotism they could hope to count on when really needed. The other was the desire among Chinese emigrants and settlers that their children would remain culturally Chinese to some degree and ensure the lines of descent for at least a few generations.[31]

Immersing myself in Chinese history has helped me understand how much China has been both repelled and fascinated by the large numbers of Chinese who have done well by living abroad, by the reasons why so many no longer wanted to return, and by what has made them replace Chinese culture with alien ways. At the same time, keeping up with the latest research on localised Chinese in each respective country around the world has also enabled me to see these communities in many lights. On the one hand, it is obvious that many Chinese have always hoped for renewed and closer links with China. On the other hand, many others, especially in North America, are ambivalent about new Chinese immigrants from Taiwan and Hong Kong. They are concerned that these new migrants seem too eager to live outside China, acquire foreign passports and still play their China cards. The range of responses to external stimuli and internal opportunities has grown so varied that, instead of becoming simpler as many had expected, the subject has become rich with contradiction and change.

I spoke of the pivotal year of 1965–1966 which led me to decide to move to Australia to continue with my research. This reminds me that, during the mid-1960s and the 1970s, there was a significant drop in the number of research projects on the Chinese communities in Southeast Asia. The London-Cornell project had turned its main attention to Hong Kong and Taiwan. New research funding on Chinese matters from the 1960s onwards had focused on the PRC itself. The Vietnam war did attract attention to the region, but there was little appeal to students of Chinese communities. Only in Australia, where concern for Indonesia and Malaysia was so intense and students from the region included so many of Chinese descent, was scholarly interest sustained. Scholars like Yen Ching-hwang, C.F. Yong, Jamie Mackie and Charles Coppel stoked the fires when elsewhere there were only embers.[32] Within the region itself, only the indefatigable Leo Suryadinata in Singapore was prepared to brave official disapproval in Indonesia to keep us informed.[33]

There were two more fundamental reasons for the shift away from research on Chinese minorities as cultural and political communities. The first was that, for reasons of security or of deep distrust, the new nation-building governments did not welcome studies about Chinese minorities that had not yet fully integrated into what was considered mainstream society. It was not only foreign scholars who were discouraged from doing so but also their own national scholars. The second was that China after 1966 was in turmoil. The Cultural Revolution turned against everyone and everything associated with the Chinese living abroad. The hostility against them included their capitalist tendencies and bourgeois ways, their seeming lack of principle, and their willingness to compromise to the point of fraternising with foreigners hostile to China. The revolutionaries distrusted even the patriotic returned overseas Chinese, and abandoned their earlier policy, which Stephen FitzGerald had so carefully analysed, of wooing them back.[34] As a consequence, there was no research on this subject within China for some 15 years. As for the Chinese outside the PRC, reactions were so negative about the consequences of the Cultural Revolution that the question of being Chinese became a painful one. Most chose to avert their eyes from the damage the revolution had done.

Once again, the Chinese overseas were thrown on their own resources. They proved that, as always, they were dynamic and well-organised enough to maximise their skills and talents. Their business activities attracted fresh attention. This, after all, was what they had always done best throughout their history outside China.[35] What was new was the reemergence of Japan as an economic power in the late 1960s. This reminded us that too much had been written about politics and culture and not enough about what so many Chinese overseas were doing every day. Their core activity, after all, has always been trading and dealing, taking risks and squeezing profits in interesting times, and plotting with ingenuity and courage when political odds were at their worst. During the 1960s, they adjusted quickly to the newly independent nations of Southeast Asia and built fresh sets of business networks for themselves. The venturesome among them also learnt to serve the global commercial and industrial cities, both in the region and beyond. Some of the more forward-looking among them had educated their children in the West, and prepared them to provide local agency services for the future borderless world.

In short, when the Suharto coup in Indonesia, the isolation of China, the large-scale naturalisation of the Chinese in the region, and the exodus of Chinese from the Indochinese states, seemed to end the *huaqiao* story once and for all, new forces had begun to create different conditions for the ethnic Chinese everywhere. With the international links they fostered, Hong Kong and Singapore provided the centres for this transformation. The Four Tigers, which had responded successfully to the Japan model, opened up new approaches for Chinese entrepreneurs to perform remarkably. A new generation of social scientists were drawn into the field and they guided research into this extraordinary phenomenon. Of those who were early to record how the Chinese were responding to opportunity, Linda Lim, Richard Robison and Yoshihara Kunio come to mind.[36] They joined the scholars who had identified Japan, South Korea and Taiwan as the new engines of growth and stimulated fresh interest in the Chinese role in Southeast Asia.

It is not surprising that this approach would link up with borderless globalization and eventually point to the diasporic features of Chinese economic activity. But the climax was yet to come. The return of Deng Xiaoping after the death of Mao Zedong was like the moment when the red-faced hero is victorious in Chinese opera. Opening up China again after 30 years of isolation led to an economic surge that surprised the world. It is enough to say that the stages of opening the front gate, then the windows and finally the front door into China determined new patterns of behaviour for Hong Kong and Taiwan Chinese, for those of Chinese descent in the region, and for those further away in the Asia-Pacific. The ramifications are so great and incalculable for the region's Chinese that scholarship has yet to catch up with the changes. Instead, they have spawned many sensational writings, ranging from chauvinistic calls for a Chinese economic commonwealth to fearful projections of a new wave of the "yellow peril".[37]

A striking part of the changes was the number of mainland Chinese who followed Taiwan and Hong Kong Chinese to North America and Australasia and chose not to return. By the middle of the 1980s, there was renewed scholarly work in China on the new *huaqiao*. This sought to connect with the work by scholars in the respective countries to which this new breed of sojourners had gone. The scale of this new activity had not been seen since the 1930s and 1940s. The enthusiasm it aroused among officials in the People's Republic was closely related to the fervent efforts to invite overseas Chinese investment into the country. To the extent that economic opportunity was open to ethnic Chinese everywhere, a new *huaqiao* syndrome was emerging.[38] Unlike the earlier focus on political identification in an anti-imperialist environment, this syndrome was linked primarily to economic activity, to the communities of Chinese acting like a trade diaspora, that is, to use Abner Cohen's much quoted words , "a *nation* of socially interdependent, but spatially dispersed communities".[38]

The flood of writings explaining China's spectacular success is now overwhelming. Most of them mention the role of the overseas Chinese in the most inclusive way, the very opposite of earlier political and sociological studies that had tended to stress the special attributes of each local community. The new writings are wont to lump Hong Kong and Taiwan Chinese together with all the others spread out over a hundred countries and territories.[40] The advances in market technologies, and the nature of credit and finance services today, have blurred earlier distinctions. Political identities are also treated as increasingly irrelevant, and old terminologies are being challenged. It should not surprise us that many social scientists are now ready to use a term like diaspora to highlight the new dimensions of the Chinese phenomenon. What is intriguing is whether this will encourage Chinese governments to affirm the idea of a single Chinese diaspora again, along the lines of the earlier concept of *huaqiao*-sojourner for all Chinese overseas. Will the use of diaspora lead even those who write outside China, notably those who write in Chinese, also to revive the more familiar term, *huaqiao*, the term that Southeast Asian governments and the Chinese there had spent so much time and trouble trying to discard for the past 40 years?

Several related developments have contributed to a potential revisionism. The three that are recognised by recent scholarship as significant are rooted in economic group behaviour, and display features of other diasporas:

1. The perception that, without official endorsement and support, the Chinese overseas have been evolving multiple levels and kinds of "informal empires" over the centuries, and that their ability to adapt modern communications technology to their use has made them a formidable power in the global economy. Behind the image of "pariah entrepreneurs" and "essential outsiders", they had established what has been called "ungrounded empires" that are both flexible and resilient.[41] Their readiness to innovate from a strong traditional trading base has given them a body of practice and theory to compete with the West, something Gordon Redding and his colleagues have elevated to what they call "Chinese capitalism".[42] This clearly supports the idea of a single Chinese diaspora.

2. The success of the First World Entrepreneurs Convention hosted by the Singapore Chinese Chamber of Commerce and Industry in 1991 has confirmed that Chinese businesses world-wide are keen to build global networks that are not less active and unified than those of the Jews and other successful migrant minorities. Three meetings of the Convention have been held since 1991, in Hong Kong, Bangkok and Vancouver. The Vancouver meeting was held at the beginning of the Asian financial crisis in 1997. In 1999, the fifth Convention in Melbourne will face its first real test.[43] There will be scholarly interest in what this represents if this scale of networking shows great vitality and produces proof of durability.

3. The third is a mutually reinforcing set of institutions going beyond business that has been reinvigorated. Examples of these are the international gatherings of surname or clan associations, the native-place societies and varieties of cultural (for example, music, performing arts, literary and scholarly) organisations that now meet regularly and are trying to strengthen Chinese social and cultural bonds.[44] These have taken modern shapes and skilfully

employ modern instruments of communication. They have cellular characteristics but are often amorphous and changeable, quick to form and disperse. There is nothing essentialist about the Chinese identity they affirm, and their members negotiate interminably as to what they want. Yet there is little doubt that they encapsulate a Chinese way to achieve an end which each group wants from time to time.

Underlying all three phenomena is the shadow of China and an unspoken assumption that China's place in the world matters to Chinese and non-Chinese alike. The growing literature on the revived links between China and the Chinese overseas needs to be taken into account, especially about those operating cross-national networks involving Chinese trading groups. From this literature, it is clear that the current salience of the term diaspora is less because of trade than because of the radical changes in global migration patterns and the impact of these changes on policies of integration and assimilation.

Of great relevance here are the tentative steps towards multi-culturalism that started in the migrant states of North America and Australasia. Its origins did not have anything to do with the Chinese. The tensions between settlers and migrants since the end of World War II had forced changes to racist and nationalist visions about assimilation. Those ideals had insisted that immigrants should assimilate towards the national majority culture as quickly as possible. But the shaming of the anti-Semites after the Holocaust, the reversal of verdicts in the Black-White civil rights actions in the United States, and the affirmation of liberal human rights values in the West, together led to a multiculturalism that was to substitute for the old "melting -pot" principle of nation-building which all nations thought they had to emulate. It is this shift in policy that cleared the way for the term diaspora to come into general use and be applied to any group that wanted it. Where the Chinese are concerned, there is a growing number in North America who admire the solidarity of the Jewish diaspora and the success of the Jewish lobby in working for the state of Israel.[45] While recognising the differences between them and the Jews, they want to follow that model where appropriate. For them, this means leaning towards the concept of a single Chinese diaspora.

The Western world has moved away from the narrow usage of the Oxford English Dictionary. Regrettably, it has spread the term so widely that past connotations no longer seem to matter. The wider its application, the more diluted and less clearly defined the term will be. In addition to the Greek and Armenian, there are now the Irish diaspora, the Afro-American, the Indian and Pakistani, the Italian, Arab, Iranian, and so on. Even the English can no longer be exempt in the former colonies where they have been the "mainstream" majority, especially if the term diaspora can now also be applied to Singaporean Chinese.[46] This could mean that the Chinese diaspora have much in common with them all, but it also suggests that the word is flexible and elastic, as so many other misleading social science and historical terms are. Does this mean we simply leave it to the scholars to determine for each diaspora what complicated ways the term might be employed? The current use of the term to mean "dispersed Chinese communities" suggests that scholars of the Chinese overseas have certainly created much new work for themselves for many years to come. The more I think about it, the unhappier I am that the term has come to be applied to the Chinese. I have used the term with great reluctance and regret, and I still believe that it carries the wrong connotation and that, unless it is used carefully to avoid projecting the image of a single Chinese diaspora, it will eventually be the source of serious misunderstanding.

Let me end with two observations. When the news of the rapes of ethnic Chinese women last May was sent around the world, human rights groups protested strongly. In addition, efforts were made to build global networks calling on all Chinese to support a political protest, and seek punishment for the perpetrators of inhuman acts.[47] Equally strong exhortations were made in Hong Kong and Taiwan, some directed against what was seen as feeble responses from the Beijing government. Eventually, Chinese people on the mainland learnt of the tragic events and many responded with understandable anger. The PRC authorities then decided to comment on the matter publicly but mildly to the Indonesian government. Within Southeast Asia, among governments more familiar with unstable Indonesian politics, there was no official response. When a few Chinese community groups around the world hold protest meetings about this tragic event, could that be a forerunner of a potential diasporic solidarity? Or does it remind us how multifarious Chinese communities have become and, therefore, how hard it will be for anyone, including Chinese governments in Beijing and Taipei, to organise a diasporic response?

My other observation follows from that question. From past experience, China received patriotic overseas Chinese support when the country was weak and under foreign attack, and when the majority outside China were recent migrants with no other loyalty. Now the differentiation among the Chinese overseas is much greater. A diaspora today would include many kinds of Chinese for whom there are specific names, or who are accustomed to distinctive identities.[48] After a century of evolution, the Chinese overseas cannot return to their relationships with the old China of the Qing empire or the Kuomintang or even the PRC of Mao Zedong. The changes have been deep. Also, China itself is deeply divided between the PRC and Taiwan, and each is able to keep its overseas supporters separate and distrustful of one another. It is not even certain that the idea of a single united China is as sacrosanct as it had been thought to be. If the past is anything to go by, it is doubtful if there will ever be a single Chinese diaspora. Much more likely is that the single word, Chinese, will be less and less able to convey a reality that continues to become more pluralistic. We need more words, each with the necessary adjectives to qualify and identify who exactly we are describing. We need them all to capture the richness and variety of the hundreds of Chinese communities that can now be found.

I began by referring to my acceptance of the word diaspora in the latest collection of essays which Wang Ling-chi and I edited. My own books have preferred "Chinese overseas", to get away from *huaqiao*, always translated as overseas Chinese, and so has ISSCO, the International Society for the Study of the Chinese Overseas which was founded after the San Francisco conference in 1992, and also the new *Encyclopaedia of the Chinese Overseas* edited by Lynn Pan.[49] However, depending on context, I still believe that the terms *huaqiao*, (*haiwai*) *huaren* and *huayi*, which I have frequently used, are valid and useful. At the conference in Manila last November which some of you attended, Teresita Ang See used the term Ethnic Chinese, and I accepted that when I gave the keynote lecture.[50]

Have I and others been inconsistent? Will we confuse our readers? I expect there will be confusion if we do not specify more exactly why we use a certain term and what is meant by it. But, after 40 years living with the problem, I no longer believe that there must be a single term for such a complex phenomenon. As an historian, I recognise that conditions change, and more names have to be found to mark the more striking changes. What we need is to be alert and open, ready to ascertain the range of meaning of each of the terms we use, and to anticipate the ramifications of using each one for a particular purpose. If we admit that there are many kinds of Chinese, and there are occasions when "Chinese overseas" may be preferred over "ethnic Chinese", or when *huayi* and *huaren* may be more accurate than *huaqiao*, then we should have no difficulty with the idea that there are times when diaspora should supersede other terms in comparative studies. After all, there are already many kinds of diasporas — an immediate example is the name of your centre of the Chinese Southern Diaspora! — and we need appropriate adjectives to pinpoint the particular kind we mean. Having moved so decisively from a rather exclusive use of the term to describe one kind of people to a promiscuous application of this same term to just about everybody, it may not be so difficult to say that there is no single Chinese diaspora but many different Chinese diasporas.

Notes

1. Anthony Reid, with the assistance of Kristine Alilunas Rodgers. Ed. 1998. *Sojourners and Settlers: Histories of Southeast Asia and the Chinese, in Honour of Jennifer Cushman.* St Leonard's. NSW: Allen & Unwin and Asian Studies Association of Australia.

2. Wang Ling-chi and Wang Gungwu. Eds. 1998. *The Chinese Diaspora: Selected Essays.* Two Volumes. Singapore: Times Academic Press.

3. "Luodi shenggen" (literally, fall to the ground, grow roots) was the title of the conference organised in San Francisco in 1991 by Wang Ling-chi and his colleagues of the University of California, Berkeley.

4. Cf. various editions of the Oxford English Dictionary before and after the 1970s with the many editions of others like Webster's Dictionary.

5. Wang Gungwu. 1981. "A Note on the Origins of *Hua-ch'iao*". In *Community and Nation: Essays on Southeast Asia and the Chinese.* Selected by Anthony Reid. Singapore and North Sydney: Heinemann Educational

Books and George Allen & Unwin for Asian Studies Association of Australia. First published in 1977 in *Masalah-Masalah International Masakini*, edited by Lie Tek Tjeng, vol. 7, Jakarta, Lembaga Research Kebudayaan Nasional, L.I.P.I., pp. 71–8.

6. The numerous publications of the scholars at Jinan University in the 1920s and 1930s are listed in Xu Yunqiao's (Hsu Yun-ts'iao) useful bibliography, *Nanyang wenxian xulu changbian*, Singapore: Dongnanya yanjiu so, 1959. Chen Da's renowned work on *qiaoxiang* (sojourner villages), *Emigrant Communities in South China*, was published in 1940, the year the Nanyang Xuehui (South Seas Society) was established.

7. Some early examples were works by J. D. Vaughan, *The Manners and Customs of the Chinese of the Straits Settlements*, Singapore, 1879; and Gustav Schlegel, *Thian Ti Hwi, The Hung League or Heaven and Earth League*, Batavia, 1866. The French scholars like Paul Pelliot and Henri Maspero paid more attention to Chinese history and culture than to the Chinese overseas, but their work did illuminate important aspects of China's relations with the Indo-China states.

8. Victor Purcell. 1951 (2nd edition 1965). *The Chinese in Southeast Asia*. London: Oxford University Press. His more detailed study of *The Chinese in Malaya*, first published in 1948, was also authoritative for decades.

9. Maurice Freedman, *Chinese Family and Marriage in Singapore* (1953) was first presented as a report to the Colonial Social Science Research Council and the Government of the Colony of Singapore. Tien Ju Kang's *The Chinese of Sarawak: A Study of Social Structure* (1953), was also an offshoot of the scholarly work supported by the British government at the London School of Economics. Both of them were students of Raymond Firth who had reported on social science research in Malaya in 1948 and prepared the ground for their field research. Other notable scholars were Alan J.A. Elliott who reported on Chinese spirit-medium cults in Singapore (1955); and Marjorie Topley whose research was on the social organisation of women's *chai-t'ang* in Singapore (1958).

10. G.William Skinner, *Chinese Society in Thailand: An Analytical History* (1957) and *Leadership and Power in the Chinese Community of Thailand*, (1958). Ithaca: Cornell University Press; Donald E. Willmott, *The Chinese of Semarang: A Changing Minority Community in Indonesia*. Ithaca: Cornell University Press, 1960. For Malaya, notable studies were by Lucian W. Pye, *Guerrilla Communism in Malaya: Its Social and Political Meaning*. Princeton: Princeton University Press, 1956, and William H. Newell, *Treacherous River: a Study of Rural Chinese of North Malaya*. Kuala Lumpur: University of Malaya Press, 1962.

The two Ph.D. theses of George H. Weightman (Cornell) on the Philippine Chinese and of Jacques Amyot (Chicago) on Chinese Familism in Manila were both completed in 1960. Also, the excellent historical study by Edgar Wickberg, *The Chinese in Philippine Life, 1850–1898*. New Haven: Yale University Press, 1965. For Cambodia, the work of William E. Willmott was done at the London School of Economics. *The Chinese in Cambodia* Vancouver: The University of British Columbia Publications Centre, 1967; and *The Political Structure of the Chinese Community in Cambodia* London: The Athlone Press, 1970.

11. For example, Tan Giok Lan, Mely, *The Chinese of Sukabumi: A Study in Social and Cultural Accommodation*, Ithaca, NY: Southeast Asia Program, Cornell University, 1961; Anthony S. Tan, *The Chinese in the Philippines: A Study of their National Awakening*. Quezon City: R.P. Garcia, 1972. The first of Leo Suryadinata's many writings dates from his Master's thesis in 1969 at Monash University, The Three Major Streams of Peranakan Politics in Java, 1914–1942 (later published in 1976). Tan Chee Beng's Cornell Ph. D. thesis was completed in 1979, later published as *The Baba of Melaka: Culture and Identity of a Chinese Peranakan Community in Malaysia*. Petaling Jaya: Pelanduk Publications, 1988.

12. Freedman's reports, Skinner's early books and the work of the Willmott brothers and Weightman are good examples of the first, and Purcell and the later Skinner of the second.

13. The first comparison was attributed to Prince Vajiravudh of Thailand. He was inspired by nationalist movements in Europe and sought to develop

Thai nationalism. From his observations of the Chinese in Thailand, he drew analogies with the Jews in Europe and embarked on educational policies that would enable the Chinese to assimilate; Walter F. Vella, *Chaiyo! King Vajiravudh and the Development of Thai Nationalism*, Honolulu: University Press of Hawaii, 1978.

14. Harry Benda had a sharp eye for Indonesian politics, especially the potential power of the indigenous Muslim traders who considered the Chinese as their rivals; *The Crescent and the Rising Sun: Indonesia Islam under the Japanese Occupation, 1942–1945*, Den Hague: Van Hoeve, 1958. Although he did not write about Chinese communities, he was keenly interested in them in Indonesia and Malaya (then West Malaysia and Singapore). We spoke several times on the subject prior to his taking the post of the first director of the Institute of Southeast Asian Studies in Singapore in 1969.

15. Some historians date this from the appointment of the first imperial Qing Consuls in Singapore from 1877; others would say that China politics began when the followers of Kang Youwei and those of Sun Yat-sen sought financial support from the overseas Chinese in Japan, Southeast Asia and North America. In terms of modern political activity involving large numbers of the *huaqiao*, I favour the latter view. For the former, see Wen Chung-chi, The Nineteenth Century Imperial Chinese Consulate in the Straits Settlements. M.A. Thesis, University of Singapore, 1964. For the latter, see Wang Gungwu, "Sun Yat-sen and Singapore", *Journal of the South Seas Society (Nanyang Hsueh-pao)*, 1959, vol. 15, no. 2; Yen Ching-hwang, *The Overseas Chinese and the 1911 Revolution, with Special Reference to Singapore and Malaya*, Kuala Lumpur: Oxford University Press, 1976.

16. Tsai Shih-shan, Henry, *China and the Overseas Chinese in the United States, 1868–1911*. Fayetteville: University of Arkansas Press, 1983. Edgar Wickberg. Ed. *From China to Canada: A History of the Chinese Communities in Canada*. Toronto: McClelland and Stewart, 1982. Charles A. Price, *The Great White Walls are Built: Restrictive Immigration to North America and Australia, 1836–1888*. Canberra: Australian National University Press,

1974. Andrew Markus, *Fear and Hatred: Purifying Australia and California, 1850–1901*. Sydney: Hale and Iremonger, 1979. Malanie Yap and Dianne Leong Man, *Colour, Confusion and Concessions: The History of the Chinese in South Africa*. Hong Kong: Hong Kong University Press, 1996.

17. Yoji Akashi, *The Nanyang Chinese National Salvation Movement, 1937–1941*. Lawrence: Center for East Asian Studies, University of Kansas, 1970. Stephen Leong Mun Yoon, Sources, Agencies, Manifestations of Overseas Chinese Nationalism in Malaya, 1937–1941. Ph.D. thesis, University of California Los Angeles, 1976.

18. Yoji (1970), pp. 113–158. At the Workshop on the History of the Malayan Emergency held at the Australian National University in February 1999, Chin Peng, not yet 16 years old in 1939, spoke candidly of his wanting to return to China to fight the Japanese during the early years of the Sino-Japanese War.

19. It was not entirely voluntary. For my benefit, my father offered to teach classical Chinese to the sons of his friends, and regularly challenged me to do better than the boys who had studied in Chinese schools and were older than me by three to four years. I managed to hold my own and, as my Chinese improved, became absorbed in more difficult literary texts.

20. This became acute during my last months back at Anderson School, Ipoh, from September 1945 to December 1946. The person who most impressed me with his growing national consciousness was the person I shared my desk with, the late Aminuddin Baki. He was, at his untimely death in 1968, the Director of Education of the Federation of Malaya.

21. My father graduated from the Southeastern University (Dongnan Daxue) in Nanjing in 1925, and had always hoped that I would go to his alma mater, renamed National Central University (Zhongyang Daxue) in 1928. He brought me to Nanjing in the summer of 1947 to sit for the entrance examinations; the results were published in the *Zhongyang Daily News* on 6th September 1947. I was admitted to the Department of Foreign Languages.

22. I was at National Central University from October 1947 to December 1948. After the Nationalist armies were defeated at the great battle of Huaihai (Northern Jiangsu) in December 1948, I decided to return to Malaya to rejoin my parents.

23. The University of Malaya, comprising the King Edward VII Medical College and Raffles College (Arts and Science), had its Foundation Day on 8th October 1949. It was the only university in British Malaya (Singapore and the newly established Federation of Malaya) and two-thirds of its students were from the Federation. Almost all its students were products of the English schools of the two territories. A clear majority was Chinese, with significant numbers of Ceylonese, Indians and Eurasians. The Malays were greatly under represented in the early years of the university's history.

24. Singapore: Donald Moore, 1959. Reprinted in my essay collection in 1992, *Community and Nation: China, Southeast Asia and Australia*, St. Leonards, NSW: Allen & Unwin, pp. 11–39.

25. I was inspired by the enthusiasm of my colleagues to edit *Malaysia: A Survey* in response to this development. This was published by Praeger in New York and Pall Mall in London in 1964.

26. Reliable accounts of the the events of 1965–1966 in Indonesia are still hard to come by. Benedict R. O'G. Anderson and Ruth T. McVey. 1971. *A Preliminary Analysis of the October 1, 1965 Coup in Indonesia*. Ithaca, NY: Modern Indonesia Project, Cornell University. Robert Cribb. Ed. 1990. *The Indonesian Killings of 1965–1966: Studies from Java and Bali*. Clayton, Vic.: Centre of Southeast Asian Studies, Monash University.

In contrast, books on the Vietnam war abound. Robert D. Schulzinger's *A Time for War: The United States and Vietnam, 1941–1975*. New York: Oxford University Press, 1997 provides a concise summary of the main features of the war.

27. "Chinese politics in Malaya", *The China Quarterly*, London, no. 43, pp. 1–30; "Malaysia: contending elites", *Current Affairs Bulletin*, Sydney,

vol. 47, no. 3, December, pp. 1–12, both published in 1970. In addition, I also commented on the May 1969 riots in West Malaysia, "Political Change in Malaysia", *Pacific Community*, Tokyo, 1970, vol. 1, no. 4, pp. 687–696.

28. The different estimates stem from the quality of Chineseness expected. Those in China measure this in terms of how much the Chinese outside are still like those in China and remain loyal to what China stands for. Those who have settled abroad are normally content if they speak the language, observe certain customs, and are able to employ Chinese ways and connections effectively. It is, however, important that their Chinese origins be respected and there is no discrimination against them as Chinese.

29. I have only anecdotal evidence, but enough to recognise among Chinese overseas the cringe that colonials have about their countries of origin. Like former colonials from Britain in Australia, there are also expressions of a similar exasperation about those who come from the "home country". In some cases with the Chinese, this is followed by self-congratulation about how well they have done outside China without China's help. These extreme attitudes may be found everywhere, not least in Southeast Asia.

30. The two best examples of Freedman's work would be *Lineage Organisation in Southeastern China* (1958) and *Chinese Lineage and Society: Fukien and Kwangtung* (1966). Other major essays have been collected in *The Study of Chinese Society*, edited by G. William Skinner (1979). Skinner also has a similarly enviable record of contributing profoundly to Chinese sociology: *Marketing and Social Structure in Rural China* (1964) and the reference work, *Modern Chinese Society: An Analytical Bibliography* (1973).

31. Wang Gungwu (1991). "Among Non-Chinese", *Daedalus, Journal of the American Academy of Arts and Sciences*, Cambridge, Mass., Spring, pp. 135–157; reprinted in *The Living Tree: The Changing Meaning of Being Chinese Today*, edited by Tu Wei-ming, Stanford University Press, 1994, pp. 127–146.

32. During these years, Yen Ching-hwang published his *The Overseas Chinese and the 1911 Revolution* (1976, see note 15); a series of essays which

were later collected in 1995 in two volumes, *Community and Politics: The Chinese in Colonial Singapore and Malaysia*, and *Studies in Modern Overseas Chinese History; and Coolies and Mandarins* (1985) and *A Social History of the Chinese in Singapore and Malaya, 1800–1911* (1986). C.F. Yong also published steadily and his essays were collected in *Chinese Leadership and Power in Colonial Singapore* (1992). His major work of this period was *Tan Kah-Kee: The Making of an Overseas Legend* (1987).

Jamie Mackie produced *The Chinese in Indonesia: Five Essays* in 1976, with an important contribution by Charles Coppel; and Coppel published his authoritative study, *Indonesian Chinese in Crisis*, in 1983. Both published several relevant essays on the subject during the 1970s and 1980s.

33. Among Leo Suryadinata's writings of this period are the following: *Indigenous Indonesians, the Chinese Minority and China: A Study of Perceptions and Policies* (1975); *Peranakan Chinese Politics in Java, 1917–1942* (1976); *The Chinese Minority in Indonesia: Seven Papers* (1978); *Eminent Indonesian Chinese; Biographical Sketches* (1978); *Political Thinking of the Indonesian Chinese, 1900–1977* (1979) and *China and the ASEAN States: The Ethnic Chinese Dimension* (1985). Several of these have been updated since first publication. He also published a series of essays which have been collected in *Chinese Adaptation and Diversity: Essays on Society and Literature in Indonesia, Malaysia and Singapore* (1993), and *The Culture of the Chinese Minority in Indonesia* (1997).

34. Stephen FitzGerald, *China and the Overseas Chinese: A Study of Peking's Changing Policy, 1949–1970*. Cambridge: Cambridge University Press, 1972.

35. Trade was what induced commoner Chinese to travel to East and Southeast Asia, firstly in small numbers before the Song dynasty (960–1276); Wang Gungwu (1958; 1998), *The Nanhai Trade: The Early History of Chinese Trade in the South China Sea*; and then in large enough numbers thereafter to be grouped as a class of *huashang* (Chinese merchants); Wang Gungwu (1990a), "Patterns of Chinese migration in historical perspective", in *Observing Change in Asia: Essays in Honour of J.A.C. Mackie*, edited by

R.J. May and W.J. O'Malley, Crawford House Press, Bathurst, pp. 33–48. (first published in Guangzhou, in Chinese, 1985); and (1990b), "Merchants Without Empire: the Hokkien sojourning communities", in *The Rise of Merchants Empires: Long-Distance Trade in the Early Modern World, 1350–1750*, edited by James D. Tracy, Cambridge University Press, pp. 400-421.

36. Linda Y.C. Lim and L.A. Peter Gosling. Eds. 1983. *The Chinese in Southeast Asia*, Vol. One: Ethnicity and Economic Activity. Singapore: Maruzen Asia. Richard Robison. 1986. *Indonesia: The Rise of Capital*. North Sydney, NSW: Allen & Unwin. Yoshihara Kunio. 1988. *The Rise of Ersatz Capitalism in Southeast Asia*. Singapore: Oxford University Press. More recently, the influential collection of essays edited by Ruth T. McVey. 1992. *Southeast Asian Capitalists*. Ithaca, NY: Southeast Asia Program, Cornell University.

37. Whether it is the Chinese economic commonwealth, Chinese Common Market, Chinese Community, or Greater China, etc., some writers envisage a coming together of all Chinese. The implication is that of a single Chinese diaspora closely linked with the Chinese mainland; David Shambaugh, "The Emergence of 'Greater China'"; Harry Harding. "The Concept of 'Greater China': Themes, Variations and Reservations" and Wang Gungwu. "Greater China and the Chinese Overseas", *The China Quarterly*, no. 136, December 1993, pp. 653–659, 660–686, 926–948.

As for fearful projections, these vary from several recent books on the overseas Chinese (*kakyo*, or *huaqiao*) by Japanese writers, to those by Sterling Seagrave, *Lords of the Rim: The Invisible Empire of the Overseas Chinese*. NY: Putnam's, 1995, to books on security threats, like that by Richard Bernstein and Ross H. Munro, *The Coming Conflict with China*. NY: A.A. Knopf, 1997.

38. This is being shaped by the sheer numbers of people involved. Also, the volume of published work on the Chinese overseas (*huaqiao-huaren*) has grown quickly, now not only in the southern provinces, but also throughout China where any connection with a local person who has migrated or settled abroad is systematically cultivated. The value of such

people to the officials of the Overseas Chinese departments has been recognised, and tracing Chinese relatives living abroad is now both a profitable as well as a humanitarian act. Research centres and units have been established by universities and societies, and serious and extensive scholarship is being done at both national and local levels. Numerous books, including volumes of collected essays, as well as dozens of specialist journals, magazines and newsletters provide increasingly well-informed studies about the Chinese world-wide. The impact this has had on China's development and on the fortunes of the Chinese overseas is yet to be accurately assessed, but a sense of intense and effective activity is unavoidable.

39. I first read this in Philip Curtin. 1984. *Cross-Cultural Trade in World History*. Cambridge: Cambridge University Press. Here I cite from Anthony Reid, "Entrepreneurial Minorities, Nationalism, and the State". In *Essential Outsiders: Chinese and Jews in the Modern Transformation of Southeast Asia and Central Europe*, edited by Daniel Chirot and Anthony Reid. Seattle: University of Washington Press. pp. 33–71.

40. This is particularly true among journalists, especially after *The Economist* gave this inclusive usage its approval, 21 November 1992. Once Hong Kong and Taiwan Chinese are so grouped, it is easy for the role of the Chinese overseas, most of them settled minorities in foreign lands who are distinguished by their ability to flourish under non-Chinese regimes, to be misunderstood and misrepresented. A clear example of this is Constance Lever-Tracy, David Ip and Noel Tracy, *The Chinese Diaspora and Mainland China: An emerging Economic Synergy*, New York, St Martin's Press, 1996, where the "Chinese diaspora" consist mainly of the Chinese of Hong Kong and Taiwan.

41. I first came to note the application of the concept of "pariah entrepreneur" to the Chinese in Southeast Asia when Joseph P. Jiang and I attended a conference sponsored by UNESCO in Singapore in December, 1963. He had just completed a thesis at Indiana University on the subject. His essay was subsequently published in the volume of the conference, *Leadership and Authority, a Symposium*. Singapore: University of Malaya Press, 1968, pp. 147–162. Most recently, the idea has been refined as

"essential outsider" (see note 39). The important point is that the identification is not a static and unchanging one, and those so called have room to negotiate how they wish to be identified from time to time. *Ungrounded empires* is the striking title of the book of essays edited by Aihwa Ong and Donald Nonini, with the subtitle *The Cultural Politics of Modern Chinese Transnationalism*. New York and London: Routledge, 1997. I explore the theme of identity in "The Study of Chinese Identities in Southeast Asia", in *Changing Identities of the Southeast Asian Chinese since World War II*, edited by Jennifer Cushman and Wang Gungwu, Hong Kong University Press, Hong Kong, pp. 1–21.

42. *The Spirit of Chinese Capitalism*. Berlin: Walter de Guyter, 1990. To what extent that capitalism could be characterised as "Chinese" is disputable, but the label has inspired many Chinese entrepreneurs to become more self-conscious and to induce later scholars to go looking for what made them uniquely "Chinese".

43. It was decided in 1998 that the secretariat of the World Chinese Entrepreneurs Convention be located at the Singapore Chinese Chamber of Commerce and Industry for a period. The choice was between Hong Kong and Singapore. So far, the Convention has been meeting outside the mainland and Taiwan, but both Beijing and Taipei organisations have been keen to bring the convention to their respective cities. When it finally meets in those two cities, the unity of the "diaspora" with the homeland would be complete. Where then is the exile or the dispersal?

44. Liu Hong, "Old Linkages, New Networks: The Globalization of Overseas Chinese Voluntary Associations and its Implications", *The China Quarterly*, no. 155. September, 1998, pp. 582–609.

45. Public debates on this subject are rare, but comparisons of "global" Chinese and Jews and their manifold activities are often made in private and at community group meetings. Unlike in Southeast Asia, the Chinese in North America are more aware of Jewish activism: Chirot and Reid's *Essential Outsiders* (note 39) is better appreciated there than anywhere else.

46. I have never seen "English diaspora" being used and always thought this was because the English know their own language best and are clear about the specificity of the word "diaspora". Now that the word has been loosened from its moorings to the extent it has, how long will it be before we speak of the English diaspora even in Canada, the United States, Australia and other parts of their own former empire?

47. The media were actively supportive in Hong Kong and Taiwan, but the most striking were those made through the Internet. Some web sites encouraged vengeful expressions, but some were positive and sought "reconciliation". For example, the World Huaren Federation whose manifesto begins with a forceful statement about the Chinese diaspora. The following quote captures the spirit of this cyberspace organisation:

> "Chinese are estimated to be living in over 136 different countries, making it perhaps the most widespread ethnic group in the world. Such diversity is indeed awe-inspiring. Yet, it is the same diversity which creates gulfs among peoples.
>
> "We often encounter Chinese-Americans or Chinese-Canadians who know or care little of their counterparts elsewhere. Such ignorance and indifference should be corrected. Our task of bringing reconciliation among Chinese-Chinese subgroups and between Chinese and non-Chinese is no doubt ladened with challenges."

48. The word Chinese does not come from any word in the language which carries the meaning of the people of the country now called China. The people have always had many names for themselves, depending on time and place, on tribal, ethnic or cultural origins, on whom they were addressing and on what occasions. The Chinese overseas around the world are the same, but even more so. "Us" has numerous sub-groups and only have a common name when faced with "Them", especially when they feel bullied or discriminated against. For example: hyphenated Chinese (Chinese-American, etc.), those distinguished by speech group and place-name (Hakka and Shanghainese), and by their foreign nationality (peranakan, or Thai, but of Chinese descent or ancestry), and so on.

49. Published in Singapore by Archipelago Press and Landscape Books, 1998; in London by The Curzon Press; and in the United States by Harvard University Press. The Chinese edition was published simultaneously by Joint Publications, Ltd. in Hong Kong.

50. The Manila meeting, in November 1998, was the Third ISSCO conference (after San Francisco and Hong Kong). The theme was Intercultural Relations and Cultural Transformation of Ethnic Chinese. My lecture was entitled, "Ethnic Chinese: The Past in Their Future".

Hong Kong and an Ambivalent Modernity*

We all know that Hong Kong, the last and one of the smallest colonies of the largest empire the world has ever seen, became in three decades one of the great cities of the world. From its entrepot commercial base, Hong Kong has become one of the key centres of global capitalism, and a model of Asian internationalism. This week, this last bastion of Western direct control over Asian people will be handed back to the country from which it was detached. For many, this is a cause for celebration.

Yet, the return to Chinese rule has given rise to skepticism, notably among three groups. The first are those who want nothing to change. Another group are those who want global supervision of every move that the Beijing authorities make. And third are those who want the future to proceed along lines determined by a Western "end of history", with the universalism and triumphalism of the West — nothing less will do. Indeed, if the future is only seen as moving from the known to the unknown, there is room

---

* This was a lecture given at a panel on Hong Kong's history at the Pacific Rim Forum's meeting on the eve of the return of Hong Kong to China. The lecture was delivered on 26 June 1997.

for doubt. But is the future really unknown? Is the so-called socialist market economy on the Chinese mainland as mysterious as it has been made out to be? Unpredictable, one must admit. Heavy-footed and clumsy, most would agree. But it is not unknown nor unknowable.

China is more open and comprehensible to the world today than it has ever been in its three and a half thousand years of recorded history. We have never had access to as much up-to date and nationally integrated data for as many parts of the country as we have today. And the situation has been improving, despite the notable breaks due to war, civil war and revolution. This is not to say that the information is always accurate or reliable, but the overall trend towards more and better information for more and more people over the past century and a half is undeniable. My historical perspective starts with this simple fact.

The questions I wish to ask are many. Why is Hong Kong so special and important? To whom is it important after the handover? To the Chinese people to whom the territory belongs? To the peoples of the regional neighbourhood? To those people in the West who see the return of Hong Kong as somehow diminishing their influence in Asia? Probably to all of them and many more varieties of people, but there isn't enough time to deal with them in my brief presentation. So I shall concentrate on the first, on the Chinese people, and specially on those in Hong Kong itself for whom obviously the handover is the most immediately important. And I do so with the perspective that we know more about the people of Hong Kong than ever before, and that what we know must give rise to hope and optimism.

I have been asked to look back and place this week's events in historical context. The theme I have chosen to encompass this large and complex task is that of modernity. China's struggle to modernise for the last 150 years has met with both failures and successes. But it learnt that, to overcome its weakness in comparison with the West, the only solution in the end was to modernise. Four ambivalent attitudes towards the modernity that the Chinese people want can been identified. They mark the hard changes that have occurred among Chinese, and provide ample proof that, tortuously and painfully, the people have opted for modernity. This is the main thrust of the century and it is something that is welcomed by most. There is always ambivalence, and even reluctance at times, but the direction towards modernity is unmistakable.

Hong Kong is that open and public stage on which continuous changes have taken place. I will suggest that its people are but part of the vanguard of change for all Chinese. Therefore, what I say about them will be relevant to changes among Chinese everywhere, and what Hong Kong people do may even be precursors to greater changes to come for the Chinese in China. Between those in Hong Kong and those in China, there are, and will always be, differences in detail and of degree. Some of the changes experienced will be telescoped, and others skipped, and yet others totally reshaped. But the course of development towards a recognisably Chinese modernity will be the same.

Let me begin at the time when, it would appear, "East is East and West is West, and never the twain will meet", when the British and the Chinese were separate if not equal. This was during the first 80 years of the colony till the early decades of the 20th century. Among the new generations of Chinese who grew up in that atmosphere, two men stand out as having taken their own somewhat different paths towards modernity. They represented the thousands of educated Chinese who had taken the first step to change China. I refer to Ng Choy, later better known as Wu Ting-fang (1842–1922), and to Sun Yat-sen (1866–1925).

They were a generation apart, but there was no question of either of them looking anywhere but to China as the object of their enduring concern. Being older and coming from a wealthy merchant family, Wu Ting-fang had more formal education in both Chinese and English. He could comfortably join his elite compatriots in the service of China despite being entrusted by the British to assist in local community affairs. He served the Qing empire loyally, but always with a mind more modern than the Manchu court would appreciate. In the end, he turned away from the imperial past to follow the younger and equally modern Sun Yat-sen when the latter returned to China in 1912 as the provisional president of that extraordinarily modern institution, the Republic of China. The institution was doubly modern because the idea of China as a nation itself was new to the Chinese people.

Sun Yat-sen's background was less rooted in Hong Kong, but he had been to Wu Ting-fang's old school, and studied medicine in the Medical College for Chinese that Wu's brother-in-law had helped to found, the precursor of the Medical Faculty of the University of Hong Kong. He came from a more humble peasant family and had studied abroad earlier. He could admire the West without having been a colonial in any way. He gained his modernity through a vision of China beyond what anyone else could imagine at the time. Probably because of that, he took the different path of rebellion and revolution.

As the two lives converged in Nanjing in 1912, they shared something in common which was probably unconscious and intangible. They had both enjoyed a British education that was filtered through Chinese spectacles so that it could serve a Chinese cause. That they had so much to offer to their country was because they had grown up when the Chinese people in Hong Kong saw themselves as separate but still culturally equal. Chinese power might have been weakened, but it was still respected. Chinese culture was treated as viable and intact by Chinese and foreigners alike. For both these men, despite or because of Hong Kong, Chinese values were confidently held in parallel with the political and philosophical ideas that they had learnt from the West. As each of them saw it, what they had learnt did not compromise their own sense of being Chinese.

There was, of course, ambivalence. For example, when Wu Ting-fang the diplomat negotiated for China's equality among the powers, he depended less on Chinese imperial rhetoric than on western law; and when he was revising the Qing criminal code, the British jurisprudence that he had imbibed turned him against Chinese methods of punishment. Similarly, Sun Yat-sen reemphasised his loyalty to Confucian values even when his nationalist ideals seemed to have been pulling him in a different direction.

For both of them, the ambivalence was easily set aside by China's revivalist cause. In short, for this stage of Hong Kong's history, the Chinese were in no way threatened by what the rich and powerful British had to offer. Instead, they saw British power as a constructive challenge. The new ideas and encouragement even protected Chinese against the depredations of a dynastic empire in decline. Although the British felt themselves superior when they watched China's descent to anarchy, most Chinese did not believe that they had much to learn from them except better means to restore their own ancient political and cultural glories. There was still enough mutual, if not always reciprocated, respect for each other for Hong Kong to play an ambivalent but valuable role in China's awakening.

These are but two examples of the many Chinese in Hong Kong during these first 80 years who considered it wholly natural to move north to work for and in China. Very few of the others, however, had careers anywhere comparable to these two. For most

Hong Kong Chinese, they could see themselves being replaced in China by those who grew up in Shanghai and other Treaty Ports. This was specially true of those who worked closely with the traditional power centres further north. By the 1920s, those from Hong Kong had become far less influential in the affairs of the new Chinese state.

The next distinctive period produced ambivalence among Hong Kong Chinese of a sharper and more contrasting kind. The ambivalence came to the fore after the 1920s, after a decade of the warlords and their multiple civil wars, and after the irresistible calls for revolution as the only way to rebuild China. Although Hong Kong was sheltered to some extent from the full force of the contradictions emerging across the border, its people did feel the emotional pull of a new national consciousness. This national pride placed its faith in modern science and democracy as something that could co-exist with their rejection of the proud traditions that had held China together for centuries. Hong Kong Chinese found their marginal position untenable. Being located in a British colony, they could choose either to join the growing China coast community and share the lives of the westerners resident there, or assert their Chineseness against the foreigners who had helped to bring China down.

In short, many Hong Kong Chinese moved from ambivalence to division in the face of China's continued impoverishment. Only the exclusiveness and superior airs of the British prevented more of them from imitating the British all the way. But for those who saw the need to make an accommodation, they had to endure the difficult position of not being accepted by both British and Chinese. It did not matter whether one was physically half-British, half-Chinese, or merely culturally so. The role of a generation of Anglo-Chinese was a painful one, and few were able to play it well with confidence.

Throughout this period of strong nationalism from the 1920s to the 1950s, only a handful could affirm their mixed identity with pride. The most outstanding of them was unquestionably Sir Robert Hotung, the successful representative of the compradores and the symbolic leader of the China coast Chinese of Hong Kong. Sir Robert Hotung was an Eurasian who made a conscious effort to remain Chinese for practical reasons, but was nevertheless able to carry his Chineseness with self-respect. But the tensions and pressures made this in-between position permanently precarious. In his own family, during his own lifetime, some chose to turn to the West wholeheartedly while others made conscious decisions to fight the Chinese cause.

After the fall of Hong Kong to the Japanese and the restoration of Chinese control over all Treaty Ports, especially that of Shanghai, the China coast Chinese had to change. The strenuous efforts at a grafting of Chinese with British values did not prevail. Few could follow the Hotung example.

But it was not all in vain. In their efforts to find an accommodation with the British and Chinese ways, a new path was found. However reluctantly or imperfectly, the Chinese who had taken this path did leave a heritage — the progressive struggle with the challenge of the modern. The path they followed led them to places where no Chinese had been before. In their own way, their lives demonstrated that China's future lay in grappling directly with the demands of modernity. Everything that happened in China during this period of invasion, civil war, and revolution confirmed that the choices before them were different kinds of modernity. There was no turning back. If Sir Robert Hotung's was not the way, the search had begun for other ways. The direction at least was clear.

Cultural separation was not the answer. What replaced it was a new kind of ambivalence which had begun in Treaty Ports like

Shanghai, but was also admired among Hong Kong Chinese. I refer to an ambivalence which sprang from not knowing which parts of the West were more modern. Young revolutionaries were impatient to master the most advanced of everything in order that China could catch up with the West as fast as possible. Hong Kong had offered progressive ideas earlier on, but young Chinese saw short-cuts in socialism and communism. They saw these as potential antidotes to what the British and their successors, the Americans, had brought to the China coast.

The new ambivalence came about because the bulk of the Chinese were led to a Western ideological heresy by Russians who were ironically considered in the West as only marginally Western. Those who chose after 1949 not to follow the new creed embraced by the Chinese Communist Party, escaped to Hong Kong in larger and larger numbers. Consciously or not, they were choosing the mainstream institutions of the capitalist West. For some 30 years, they watched the fires of an earlier nationalism quenched in Taiwan, and smothered by a romantic internationalism on the mainland. As most of them struggled to survive in the slums and hillsides of Hong Kong, they absorbed the lessons of a mature modernity. This took the shape of an orderly and relatively honest administration, an arcane but fair system of law that protected private property, and economic and financial organisations which rewarded the skilled and the enterprising.

Was this what modernity is really about? If they did not first believe it, most of them were soon convinced that what they encountered in Hong Kong were better ways towards modernity than anything they had experimented with in China in the past. Hong Kong itself was changing. No longer was it the British colony exclusively peddling British ways as it had done before 1941. It had become the front line for a globalising capitalism fighting a desperate battle in Asia against communism. No one could be certain then who would win, but the struggle ensured that there were plenty of new opportunities, and that there was access to capital and credit. These enabled every Hong Konger who dared to do so to come forward and take the necessary risks in a favourable environment.

A new community was formed, one that was infused with people from all over China, notably Shanghainese and more Chaozhou and Fujian natives, and also foreigners from East and West who came to seek their fortunes. Hong Kong was no longer the home of the Cantonese. The full story of the hundreds of thousands of Chinese who entered Hong Kong during these decades has yet to be told. I dearly hope that this generation of historians will flesh it all out soon. What I understand of the transformation is best described through the products of Hong Kong education during the first decade after 1949. That was the generation which grew to prominence 30 years later in the 1980s and 1990s. When they were still at school in the 1950s, there was still a major divide between those who went to essentially English schools and those who went to schools that taught entirely in Chinese. The two sets of schools offered different paths to modernity, one that was clearly modelled on what was regarded as standard and good in Britain, and the other inheriting the traditions of national education developed in China.

I have quite deliberately taken my final examples of ambivalent modernity from the two contrasting groups. I shall offer a simplified profile of the two in order to make a more general point about the new modernity that most Chinese now face. The first group consists of those who, whether local-born or immigrant main-landers, tended to identify with China and accept its past efforts at modernising as their starting-point. The second is largely re-presented by those who recognised the limits of traditions both past and present, and were willing to look more openly outwards in order to broaden Chinese horizons further and enhance a more consistently modern framework.

Let me begin with the first group. For most of them, their backgrounds include some immersion in Chinese schools, but many had spells in Hong Kong's elite English schools as well. The entrepreneurs and businessmen among them were careful to be politically correct in a British colony, but never lost their close links with China. The more politically active, however, consciously opted to be anti-colonial and identified with things Chinese. The most prominent of them stayed close to the wider Chinese community. Many remained in business, or fields like education, trade unionism, and social welfare, and rose to leadership positions. Others, however, were prepared to work for companies and agencies of the People's Republic of China in Hong Kong, and some rose high after decades of loyal service. Despite their common education backgrounds, they were led to different personal choices and worked in different circles. They thus gained contrasting perspectives on Hong Kong's future.

After the Joint Declaration, and when the crunch came after the Tiananmen tragedy, a number of them took a sharply different road. They did so not by leaning towards the British, but by confidently affirming that they were modern and patriotic Chinese who should be engaged in the betterment of China itself. Indeed, many were critical of the government on the mainland and became supporters of democracy. They were prepared to join people from other more obviously westernised backgrounds who had come to their political positions by totally different routes. I shall not dwell here on the contrasting styles of the supporters of democracy in Hong Kong. Instead, I wish to underline a more telling point. What divided them politically from those who remained trusting of the regime in China may reveal ambivalence in attitudes, but Hong Kong had produced in them all a natural and unselfconscious commitment to modernity that is quite new. Their differences stemmed from the choices they had made when they were young, choices that were essentially rational and each guided by an equally strong desire to be modern. This desire was further enhanced by their exposure to the open international economy that had impinged so strongly on Hong Kong for half a century.

The second group, who are skeptical of tradition and more willing to learn from the West, include descendants of old Hong Kong families open to decades of British influence, and also the better-educated immigrants from various parts of China, notably from Shanghai and other Treaty Ports. It is not, however, family backgrounds that define their modernity. Perhaps it is the China coast ambience, and the fact that most of them received an English-language education, that give their ideas of modernity a flavour of their own. They pursued notably different careers. Many went into Hong Kong's public service or the professions. Others sought modern management training and joined the larger commercial and industrial establishments.

Of the former, many would have studied in the best Hong Kong English schools, with some going on to the University of Hong Kong when it was still elitist and strongly attached to the values of Oxford and Cambridge. They would tend to remain true to that heritage, but would also have the cultural skills to move easily in modern Chinese circles. The latter are more likely to be deeply influenced by looking outwards at more Anglo-American horizons and, through their wider business networks and connections, become more truly international. In both groups are to be found the convergencies that one might be led to expect from a modernising China and the already modern English-speaking West. Their ambivalence comes not from being in an in-between position looking both east and west. Instead, both enjoy the comfortable high ground of knowing how the West works, and are ambivalent only about how much to adapt when they return to face the new forces that are now modernising China itself. The challenges of Hong Kong that had engaged them when young have placed them in the unique positions they now enjoy. It is again Hong Kong under a different sovereignty that will point to a new stage of modern Chineseness yet to be shaped.

Hong Kong has moved during the past century and a half from unequal separateness to insecure cultural conjunctions and then, from the lessons learnt, moved further to a growing poise and confidence towards all things modern. Through that period, it has changed from a small generator pumping Western ways into China into a powerhouse of the modern and the cosmopolitan that assisted the recent transformation of South China.

In the examples I have given above, we see a silent drama of Anglo-Chinese adaptation. In the face of Chinese cultural decay and Western dominance, different roles have been tried. And each role has helped to prepare that which followed. As the play unfolded in all its violence, the message became clearer. The thousands, even millions, who charged into an unknown future in Hong Kong, with moderns to the left of them and moderns to the right of them, have completed their historic and heroic task. The Hong Kong Chinese are now modern not necessarily in the way the West had expected, nor in the way their mainland countrymen might have wanted. But it is now the only part of China which has achieved this without major interruptions. The ambivalent progressions from Wu Ting-fang and Sun Yat-sen to the likes of Sir Robert Hotung, and now to the two contemporary groups who will remain after the handover, have been continuous. No other comparably modern Chinese community exists. The Hong Kong Chinese seem now ready for the last act, in which they offer their own blend of modernity to all Chinese who might want it.

The Shanghai-Hong Kong Linkage[*]

In 1997, it was the Hong Kong handover, in 1998, the resurgence of Shanghai. This coupling is no accident if we see how the two cities are linked in history. It is clear that how Shanghai came to serve the world for the first half of the 20th century, and how Hong Kong came to do the same for the second half, are two of the most important stories of international Asia this century.

I love comparing two cities, whichever two cities you can think of. During the ten years I lived in Hong Kong, the favourite comparison was between Hong Kong and Singapore. When I moved to Singapore, not surprisingly, there was equal attention being paid to Hong Kong as the city for Singapore to compete with, or to learn from. From time to time, the leaders of each city would graciously refer to the other as a city that their people might emulate. And I imagine that comparisons between those two cities will go on for a long time to come.

Few have compared Hong Kong to Shanghai in a similar way, that is, as two cities that were equally important and clearly

---

[*]This was a lecture given on 24 September 1998 at a panel organised by the Pacific Rim Forum in Shanghai.

comparable. For the first part of this century, it was the cosmopolitan Shanghai that was the glittering pearl of the Orient, or Paris of the East. Some also saw it as the heart of a powerful Anglo-American-Japanese condominium that had the power to move people and events in China. British Hong Kong, in contrast, was relatively parochial and could only draw inspiration from Shanghai and import its modern ideas and practices. To most Chinese, and probably to most foreigners as well, Hong Kong was but a pale shadow of Shanghai.

Then, after 1949, that was radically changed. The government in Beijing did not wish Shanghai's foreign ways to remain dominant in the new China that the communists were building, and began to disperse its wealth and talent to the interior. Those in Shanghai who could get away, but who did not want to go to either Taiwan or the United States, went in large numbers to Hong Kong. Half a century of developments later, the earlier position had been totally reversed. Hong Kong is now the great open city, the heart of international trade and finance. It seems to be Hong Kong's turn to become Shanghai's teacher. The pendulum has swung to Hong Kong. With the new century coming soon, the question that is often asked is, will the pendulum swing back to Shanghai again?

Before I try to answer that question, I want to give you a bit more history. How many of us remember that Macau was the precursor of Hong Kong? If you do, you will note that British administration of Hong Kong was shaped by the Portuguese enclave's 280 years of experience of dealing with the Chinese from the middle of the 16th century to the 1840s, as well as British frustrations with the Canton system for more than a century. It was by learning from the unhappy Macau-Canton experience that Hong Kong evolved the way it did under British rule. In turn, the first twenty years of Hong Kong's history was important for

Shanghai. It was the Hong Kong base which kicked start the unique arrangements for what has been called the semi-colonial "leased territories" of Shanghai. For at least one generation, Cantonese compradores from Hong Kong serviced British enterprises in Shanghai. Many of them stayed on and provided support for a two-city axis that helped the British to dominate the China coast for the rest of the century.

Let me go one step further. Hong Kong was under direct British control while the "settlement" in Shanghai was shared, first with the French, then with the Americans and later with the Japanese as well. Whenever there was trouble in Shanghai, whether it be the Small Dagger and the Taiping rebellions, or later, with warlords fighting one another and nationalists at war with the Japanese or the communists, the British always had shelter in Hong Kong. In comparison, the French base was much further away in Saigon and the Americans had none until they took Manila at the end of the century. The real threat to British dominance came eventually from the Japanese. Their proximity to the Chinese mainland gave them a great advantage over all other powers. They could only be constrained, for a short while, through the Anglo-Japanese alliance. But Hong Kong, together with Singapore, could still provide some relief and protection for British interests in Shanghai.

Each of the two cities has had its historians, but the story of what they achieved in tandem still waits to be told. This is obviously not the place to do that. In any case, as we are gathered in Shanghai to observe what this city is going through to regain its former glory, I feel our attention should be directed to what has driven the two cities from within. In particular, two questions remain of interest till this day. The first is, how did the way the cities were governed affect the residents' ideas of governance? The second is, how did Chinese reaction to foreign rule lead to various forms of nationalism? These two questions bound the two cities together more than has been acknowledged in the past. They seem to me also to be deeply relevant to the roles which the two cities will play in the next half century.

By governance, I include not only institutions but also ideas of what constitutes good government. Sun Yat-sen in 1923, in a speech to the students at the University of Hong Kong, spoke of his memories of Hong Kong administration during his youth. He was a medical student in Hong Kong from 1887 to 1892, but had also been at high school there, and had been in and out of the colony many times both before and after those formative years of his life. His praise for the quality of Hong Kong government is credible. It reflects the fact that, for all its limitations, the structure of administration was superior to any he had seen in China, Macau, and Hawaii, and that memory had remained strong in his mind more than thirty years later. By the 1920s, Sun Yat-sen had been to Shanghai several times, but I am not aware of any praise he had for that city's mixed form of government. He had also travelled to Europe, Japan and North America, and presumably was suitably impressed by some of the most modern cities of the time. But that did not seem to have diminished his appreciation of good government in Hong Kong.

There were other Hong Kong Chinese of his time who supported this view. Among those who had also been abroad, one is known to have influenced him directly. This was Ho Kai, who founded the medical school in which Sun Yat-sen studied. Ho Kai was both a doctor and a lawyer and had served on the Hong Kong Legislative Council for more than ten years. Between 1887 and 1900, he and his friend Hu Liyuan wrote their reformist proposals which centred on governance based on the welfare of the people. They praised the legal and administrative system which supported private enterprise and gave the merchant class freedom to develop their skills and make wealth for the country. They even defended British expansion into Asia and saw that as a progressive force against Chinese imperial and feudal practices.

No less interesting were two men who had worked most of their lives in 19th century Shanghai, but whose familiarity with British methods of administration in Hong Kong led them also to recommend reforms to Chinese governance along recognisably British lines. I refer to to Wang Tao (1828–1897), who came from the county of Kunshan near Shanghai, and worked in this "foreign" city for about fourteen years before being forced to move to Hong Kong. In Hong Kong, where he lived for over twenty years, he is well-known for having worked with James Legge on his translation of the Chinese classics. But Wang Tao's contributions to journalism made a greater impact on his times, and in the newspapers he founded in Hong Kong, he often wrote about the norms of municipal government which no Chinese city could match. The other person was Zheng Guanying (1842–1922), a Cantonese who travelled the other way, from Hong Kong to Shanghai. He grew up in Macau and Hong Kong, and became a young compradore of Butterfield and Swire in Shanghai in 1860. He began writing and publishing his views three years later when he was only twenty-one, but his best-known work was the collection of essays entitled *Shengshi weiyan* (Warning Words for Prosperous Times). On one of his trips home, he met Sun Yat-sen and shared each other's views on the need for reforms. Even Mao Zedong claimed to have been influenced by *Shengshi weiyan* when he was a student.

With both Wang Tao and Zheng Guanying, their reformist drives came from seeing how the two cities were governed. I am unable to determine which city influenced which part of their new interpretations of political responsibility. In areas of applied science, technical education, and international law, Shanghai would have made the greater contribution through the initiatives taken by the Jiangnan Arsenal to bring in foreign experts to translate Western works into Chinese. But where an integrated and consistent system of government was concerned, I should think that Hong Kong had a much greater effect on them than the often confusing cluster of control methods employed to satisfy different masters in Shanghai.

In short, two models of progress presented themselves, one foreign ruled and the other a volatile mix that offered political freedom to an extent never known before. The latter, the city of Shanghai, was so dynamic that it had overshadowed Hong Kong before the end of the 19th century. But not before Hong Kong had contributed to the brand of nationalism which Sun Yat-sen and his secret society friends of Hong Kong, Macau and Guangzhou (Canton) began to formulate. The origins of this nationalism are many. They can be traced back to humiliation at China's multiple defeats by European imperialists, or to discrimination experienced by overseas Chinese, or to deep-seated hatred of Manchu rule in South China, or even to specific hurts that aroused young intellectuals to retaliate. And, not least, this nationalism arose because there was no faith in the Qing empire's ability to provide a more modern government. This last pointed to a contrast that was more sharply felt with British rule in Hong Kong. It was no accident that the opening waves of nationalist revolution against the Qing dynasty began with Sun Yat-sen and that his first surge of support came from Hong Kong.

Clearly Hong Kong led Shanghai in giving initial shape and voice to Chinese nationalism, but Shanghai was not far behind. Once the call was made and new nationalists flocked to Shanghai, the latter city responded quickly. The freer and more diverse city attracted more brain power and more entrepreneurship to push the cause to a much higher pitch. The wealth-making talents enabled the city to grow at twice the rate of Hong Kong by the end of the century. The range of new work opportunities drew a young and adventurous population from a much greater hinterland, all of coastal China to its south and north, the middle and lower Yangtse river valleys, and the major cities of the interior. I can envisage the flood because I saw the same phenomenon occur in the 1980s and early 1990s in Hong Kong when the same pull was exercised on all the mainland cities and provinces. The major difference was that Hong Kong in the 1990s had well-developed administrative controls, whereas the institutions of Shanghai in the first half of the century were free but chaotic.

Of course, there was a broader range of differences. Where Hong Kong remained a trading centre for the region that also serviced British strategic interests, Shanghai had gradually become an industrial and financial city. Foreign interests had become increasingly powerful and Chinese investors found the competition too strong. Thus in Shanghai, there were good reasons for shrill nationalist responses. It was but an easy leap from anti-Manchu displays to questions about exploitative imperialism, about foreign companies growing at the expense of local enterprises. The new elites joined the displaced old elites to declare that moderate reforms were ineffective and the time had come for a broader-based revolution. Frustration and impatience with corrupt warlord governments led to a powerful coming together of the interests of both capitalists and workers alike.

Within a few years of the Republic being founded in 1912, the nationalist pendulum had decisively swung to Shanghai. The city was not only much richer, but it had seized the political lead as well. Sun Yat-sen's nationalists moved north to use it for their financial and intellectual base, and dozens of new political parties were launched there, not least the Chinese Communist Party in 1921. The national capital, Beijing, in contrast, was too constrained by a central government hostile to political change, while Hong Kong had become far from where the action was. The exodus of scholars, teachers, artists, and journalists from other cities to Shanghai was just the tip of the iceberg. Shanghai was the major centre of free and open modern governance. The people there gave the warmest support to the May Fourth movement of 1919, and provided the spearhead of labour revolt during the May Thirtieth incident in 1925. The city was seen as the vanguard of all progressive thought. By the end of the 19th century, it had also became the publishing and performing centre for everything important, and all manuscripts and artistic offerings needed to go via Shanghai to ensure that they were distributed nation-wide.

Rapid progress has its price. There was a huge irony that China's most enlightened and cosmopolitan city should be the most nationalistic, and its richest and best developed city the most revolutionary. Such a contradiction could not last. The popular acceptance of class struggle rhetoric among the educated young and the unskilled workers of Shanghai led easily to the radicalisation of politics in the city. In defence, merchant interests acted to divide the powerful Nationalist Party, the Guomindang, as its armies marched towards Shanghai in 1927. And how quickly the pendulum swung again. The right-wing of the Nationalists led by Chiang Kai-shek turned against its communist and other left wing comrades within the city. At this point, leading Shanghai businessmen, adventurers and secret societies combined forces to help carry out that purge. Almost overnight, the large Chinese parts of this free city became politically one of the most repressive, and drove the radical forces inland or back to Hong Kong.

Were it not because of the foreign business interests in Shanghai, an aggressive economic nationalism would have seized the city by 1930, two decades earlier than it eventually did. But the Nationalist government in Nanjing needed the revenues to fight its civil war against their Communist enemies, and sought Anglo-American support against the rising ambitions and power of Japan. Japanese aggression in 1928 in Shandong and in 1931 in Manchuria, and in Shanghai itself, was the prelude to outright war. The warning bells alerted those who could leave to secure a refuge in Hong Kong. Thus were the fortunes of the two cities entwined again. It was not the full swing of the pendulum, but the preparations were wise. By 1937, when the Sino-Japanese War started, those companies which had an additional base in Hong Kong fared better than those which did not, at least for four years. Eventually, both cities were swollen with refugees from poverty and destruction. Neither could escape the full consequences of what had become a world war.

The two cities were complementary from the start where British business interests were concerned. But as other foreign capitalists worried about losing control in Shanghai, they too fell back on Hong Kong for better protection against the growing Chinese reaction to foreign governance.

Among the Chinese themselves, they remained ambivalent between the two cities. The Nationalists were embarrassed by the foreign presence, not only because of abstract issues of sovereignty, but also because their opponents used both cities to organise against their regime. The new Chinese bourgeoisie, on the other hand, were caught between dependence on foreign capital and technology, and the unfair advantage that their foreign competitors had under international or British governance. Nevertheless, Chinese entrepreneurs took every opportunity to advance their business interests wherever they could. They had learnt to appreciate what a superior legal system could do for them.

The complementarity which the cities enjoyed as the two pillars of the China coast for the period between the Great Depression after 1929 and the fall of Nationalist China in 1949 had been forced on them. But there were benefits. The enforced condition brought them mutual support and a new degree of inter-dependence. It did not matter which was richer, which was better governed, and whose capitalists were the better models for China. What mattered was the intertwining of fates, the closer links among their community leaders that made the cities more responsive to each other's needs and more willing to cooperate in defence of their common interests. And perhaps never more so than the years before all this came to an end, the years after the end of the Second World War.

For four years, from 1945 to 1949, the two cities were poised between opportunity and disaster. On one side was the prospect of a long-drawn civil war between Chiang Kai-shek and Mao Zedong. On the other was the recovery of a vast market for people deprived of basic manufactures for eight long years. The reality gave no reason for optimism. Runaway inflation threatened to destroy the small surviving middle class in both cities. Uncontrolled migrations from the impoverished countryside brought disease, food shortages and social unrest. Also, by that time, Shanghai had returned to full Chinese control while Hong Kong had begun to wonder how long more it would last as a British colony. Yet, in the midst of so much uncertainty, the social and economic bonds established earlier stood the test and showed their strength and resilience. Chinese, Eurasians and Westerners alike combined to protect what they still had and started rebuilding their businesses where they could. It was a brief window of opportunity that served them well when the gates slammed close on Shanghai and a small door was left ajar in Hong Kong after 1949.

I was witness to some of the swift transfers of people and capital from Shanghai to Hong Kong during this period, and saw how it continued for another few years into the mid-1950s. That was a remarkable story of a successful relocation of scarce capital and skilled human resources. It was certainly the secret of Hong Kong's eventual success.

But to return to governance and Chinese reactions, what a contrast of fates for the two cities. We all know what befell Shanghai when the young revolutionaries who had been driven out of the city in the late 1920s came back to reclaim their sovereign rights. Their underlying nationalism, which had been nurtured in Shanghai, led them to cut it off from most of the world. Mao Zedong, whose political career had begun there when the Communist Party was founded in 1921, now turned the city inward to service the modernisation of the great Chinese interior. However well-intentioned, the policy was disastrous for Shanghai because without succour from the world outside, the city was much diminished in every respect.

Hong Kong as the only outside link became vital to China. With the end of all private trading with the outside world, China essentially returned to the past and recreated Hong Kong as a throwback to the Macau-Canton system that had irked the West for centuries. Paradoxically, this tiny door that was left open became something much more than either Macau or Canton ever was. There are many reasons why this happened. Obviously, this was another time, and thus another story. The world had changed beyond recognition. But two reasons stand out which are relevant today.

The first reason is that Hong Kong's ties with Shanghai ensured that much of the latter's resources were transferred to Hong Kong. The industrial and financial skills transplanted well. The international connections were resumed quickly. The Shanghai bourgeoisie who chose to stay cooperated with Hong Kong commercial interests, and the fusion of the twin sets of mercantile values thrived in the new environment. Despite the continuous uncertainty which accompanied the remaking of Hong

Kong as a cosmopolitan city in Shanghai's image, the people who came by the hundreds of thousands from the mainland built their own new world under foreign rule.

Again, we return to the question of governance. The contrast between rigid central planning and near totalitarian control over personal lives on the one hand, and open and free market enterprise on the other, has rarely been as great as what Hong Kong people experienced for some 30 years after 1949. Along the narrow frontiers between capitalism and communism, a new generation of Chinese discovered themselves. They found that they could put up with foreign rule when it was relatively just and honest. They mastered the principles of law and administration which could make their society prosper, in contrast to those which impoverished their countrymen across the Shum Chun river.

Most remarkably, among them were voices which cannot fail to remind us of the writings of a hundred years earlier. From the patrician class came words which remind us of the sober advice of Dr Ho Kai and his friend Hu Liyuan. From the new literati versed in the latest political and philosophical tracts, one hears similar voices to the warnings of Wang Tao and Zheng Guanying. Like these two when they first saw the bustling Shanghai of the mid to late 19th century, the young elites today are challenged and greatly excited. And, not least, especially among those who escaped from regimented towns or oppressive work brigades across the border, one can hear calls for change in Shanghai akin to the revolutionary slogans that Sun Yat-sen had introduced to Hong Kong. These echoes are hopeful for the 21st century, but they are also sad because they remind us that the governance so many had wished for is yet unfulfilled for their country.

Thus we are now on the eve of the moment when the pendulum swings back from Hong Kong to Shanghai. Does it work like that, like some superior mechanism timed to return? Of course not. A politically united China is now stronger than it has been for 200 years. An economically vibrant China gives more respect to its merchant classes than it has ever done in its entire history. But there is also a culturally feeble China, one that is no longer confidant of its own traditions. Hong Kong has already ceded leadership to Shanghai in industrial growth. Its trading advantages have also been countered by Shanghai's superior location as the dragon's head of the mighty Yangtse valley. If its superiority as a financial centre is also challenged before long, what then can it offer to Shanghai?

I suggest two things, both of which can be traced back to the 150 years of a shared history. The first is the example of stable governance through a strong legal system. In Hong Kong, the Chinese have mastered a British art by decades of selective adaptation. They have avoided the extremes of cultural denial that the Shanghainese have had to endure, and they have also avoided mere imitation of foreign models. In their unique way, they have become the one coherent group of Chinese who can claim to inherit the mantle of those people of Shanghai who first learnt how to handle the modern world. The Hongkongers now have something to bring back to Shanghai.

The second is that complementarity which served both cities well whenever one was in danger. History shows that Shanghai was the more volatile and surprisingly, given its great vitality, the more vulnerable. Has this underlying condition changed? For the 50 years of autonomy guaranteed to Hong Kong, perhaps not. If so, it is because Hong Kong's governance has been an advantage. It has the settled strength of continuity and proven viability which Shanghai has never enjoyed. As long as this is true, the maturing political culture that Hong Kong has to offer may be its greatest gift to Shanghai when the pendulum does swing back.

Transforming the Trading Chinese*

When the first Asian businessman was listed among the world's billionaire entrepreneurs, the news was received as if he had been awarded a Nobel Prize in business. Soon after, the questions became more boastful, even blase, "How many will we get this year this year and how many more the next?" These entrepreneurs are socially respected and popularly admired. Many have greatly improved their access to power and are even regularly consulted by political leaders both within and outside their countries. It is hard to believe that, not that long ago (in some places, early this century and in others, much later), merchants in Asia were despised by those in power.[1] For hundreds of years in China, merchants were carefully controlled and denied entrance into the political establishment. In India, theirs was an inferior caste. As for Southeast Asia, they were hardly mentioned in their own historical records.

---

*An earlier version of this essay was published in the *Far Eastern Economic Review*, Asian Millennium, Part Two, 10th June 1999, as "Long Path to Power", pp. 40–44.

A remarkable change occurred during the 20th century. The entrepreneurial classes in Asia have now established a role in society and politics unthinkable at the beginning of the millennium. Many have become essential today to systems of power in countries where they had been subject to the whims of kings, nobles and the literate elites since time immemorial. That transformation is specially dramatic in Southeast Asia. After centuries spent struggling vainly for status, indigenous merchants have transformed their relations with those in power. They still include many who have started from humble beginnings, but many more are better educated and have received a variety of training. And they are increasingly expected to play public roles, some of which would prepare them to be partners in the power structures of the next millennium.

How did that happen?

From the first millennium of the modern era, the coastal peoples of South and West Asia (largely from India, Persia and later the Arabian states) took the lead to trade with both mainland Southeast Asia and the islands of the Indonesian archipelago en route to Chinese ports.[2] Their reach was remarkable when one considers the shipping and navigational conditions of the time, but perhaps their most enduring achievement was to show how trading initiatives could leave great cultural artifacts in their wake. We still point to the early monuments of Borobodur and Angkor Wat that show influences from these merchants who came by sea. But there were also persistent ideas and institutions of religious, political and artistic life that have enriched the region as a whole. The best examples would be the nature of kingship and the role of ritual, the spread of Hinduism, Buddhism and Islam, and the marvellous stories adapted from the Ramayana and Mahabharata. Such achievements testify to the way commercial vigour could fashion and enhance civilisation when trade flourished freely and attracted the active participation of local elites.

Maritime commerce in Asia, however, had to contend for long centuries with agricultural empires whose interests lay elsewhere. It was challenged by states which placed stability over mobility and which were engrossed with defending land borders from nomadic confederations greedy for their wealth. Both China and India established value-systems that neglected the sea and asserted the primacy of politics, and these influenced the values of their neighbours in mainland Southeast Asia. Over time, even the successive polities in Java, the Central Vietnam coast and the Menam valley that profited from the trade brought to their ports adopted similar prejudices against trade. Like in China, Southeast Asian rulers were wary of their own traders and preferred that their officials dealt directly with foreign merchants. In this way, they were inhibited from creating their own long-distance trading empires that could take advantage of the free flow of sea-going commerce.

Although the conditions for a maritime civilisation were absent locally, the trade through the region continued to grow during the second millennium. For such trade to be successful over a sustained period, there needed to be political support for armed shipping and a commitment to mercantile values that encouraged risk-taking for high profits. A thousand years ago, only the Arabs and Muslim South Asians who led the trade with China had such a background and their efforts enabled them to extend their enterprises into the Malay archipelago. Eventually, they stimulated Chinese merchants themselves to develop better ocean-going shipping to trade in the region as well.[3]

During the 10th century, the briefly independent kingdoms in southern China, in Guangdong, Fujian and Zhejiang provinces, welcomed that trade and opened a new era of maritime activity for the Chinese. This trade was built around a network of official relations with Champa and the Khmer empire on the mainland, and the Srivijayan port cities of Sumatra and the Malay peninsula that later came under the dominance of Javanese Majapahit. The trade also opened up relations with parts of Borneo and the Philippine islands. With the support first of the Southern Song dynasty (1127–1279) and then of the Mongol Yuan dynasty (1260–1367) officials in southern China, a strong Chinese trading presence was established in all the littoral states of the South China Sea.[4] It did not challenge the through trade which the South and West Asians had pioneered and still dominated, but it made inroads into the intra-regional and entrepot trade.

Wherever there was rivalry and competition, conflicts were inevitable, and various Chinese and Muslims were involved in the wars of Champa, Srivijaya and Majapahit. But records are scanty, being largely Arabic and Chinese rather than preserved in local language sources, and all are short on details about the volume of the growing trade and the specifics of the serious disputes that arose from time to time among local rulers and port officials. What is clear, however, is that, on the eve of the arrival of European armed merchants during the 16th century, a number of large emporia had been established in Southeast Asia which provided the early Portuguese, Spanish and Dutch officials and traders with the basic conditions for commercial expansion.[5]

Thus the first half of the 2nd millennium saw local trade develop alongside a larger through trade created by merchants from the Indian Ocean. The fact that there was no East Asian counter response was not due to the lack of naval strength. Only just a century before the coming of the first Portuguese in 1508, the Chinese of the Ming dynasty (1368–1644) demonstrated that they had the power by sending out the seven great naval expeditions of 1405–1433 led by the Muslim Chinese Admiral Zheng He

(Cheng Ho). These did not, however, reflect any change of Ming anti-mercantile policy. On the contrary, the expeditions were an affirmation of the dynastic concern to monopolise all foreign trade and keep it out of private Chinese hands.[6] This was a policy that the Ming rulers maintained for nearly 200 years. It was not until 1567, in the face of intensified maritime trade off the China coasts spearheaded by the Portuguese that the policy was relaxed and some Chinese merchants were officially permitted to trade abroad. Still, unlike the Europeans and some Southeast Asian rulers, and more like the isolationist rulers of India and Japan, the Chinese gave their traders no naval support. This left the region open to further external penetration by the West, which was not long in coming. By the end of the 16th century, both the Spanish and the Dutch had begun to intensify the European rivalry that dominated economic growth in Southeast Asia for the next three centuries.

What is even more important was that, for the Europeans, a fundamental shift in the relationship between trade and power had begun. This had its beginnings in the Mediterranean world of trading empires. In contrast, all attempts to build trading empires in Southeast Asia, whether by the Javanese, the Chams, the Khmers, the Malays or the Thais, had been futile. This had been due to the fact that, for their rulers, it was political power that made trading wealth possible, never the other way round. This had also been true of other polities elsewhere in Asia, strikingly so in India and China. It was political power that generated and guaranteed wealth. Rich merchants could be instruments of that power, but their wealth did not translate into power. Without legal protection of private wealth, confiscation was an often repeated means of ensuring that great wealth did not build up a rival power base. Thus, such wealth was always peripheral to political power.

The Europeans were to offer a different model. They brought not only stronger ships and new methods of naval warfare, but also represented different political systems. When they first arrived, their distance from their home bases on the shores of the Atlantic Ocean made them cautious and vulnerable. Nevertheless, they were strong enough to establish fortified ports to secure their trading needs, especially in Southeast Asia. In succession, the bases were erected as extensions of those in India and the African coasts. The larger ones that remained secure for centuries were those in Goa, Melaka, Macau, Manila and Batavia.[7] Other attempts to found new ones in Taiwan, Vietnam and the Malay peninsula were aborted, but the quest for more bases continued well into the 18th century, culminating in the major British advances in India and then in Penang in 1785. By that time, the French were also pushing into the region, and succeeded in establishing their foothold in the Indochinese peninsula at the beginning of the 19th century.[8]

On the surface, the European merchants and officials acted like local potentates in using political and naval power to gain trading wealth. In fact, they knew that the nature of political power at home was changing. The most advanced in directly linking political and merchant power had been the Dutch. The merchants who managed their East India Company represented the new political spirit of participation and responsibility that marked the prelude to the citizen and nation states that ultimately transformed European politics. They formed the bourgeois class and established the nexus with professional politicians that have characterised modern governance ever since.

Throughout Europe in the 18th and 19th centuries, governments were being modified by mercantilist ideas. Even the imperialism that arose from the far-flung territories controlled by the Spanish, the British and the French was based on institutions developed out of those ideas. The state would marshal its resources to support industrial capitalism and the capitalists who competed successfully against their foreign rivals were rewarded for their contributions to national power. It was not for nothing that imperialism came to be linked to the capitalism that began to flourish following Western advances into Asia.[9]

There was, of course, a transitional phase in this realignment of the power balance between European merchants and the political establishment. Stories of the extravagant displays of wealth by company officials and country traders in India and Southeast Asia during the 17th and 18th centuries showed that European merchants were willing to follow local practices because such displays bought status where wealth alone could not be translated into power. But the evolving European political system offered the newly rich a share of power and positions of trust. There were also other dramatic changes. The industrial revolution in Britain gave even greater advantages to the maritime power that had introduced global trade to all parts of the world. The emergence of a series of nation-states in Europe after the French revolution and the empire of Napoleon led these states to build rival empires all over Asia and Africa. Trade had openly become the hand-maiden of political expansion, and trading wealth began to influence the political arena more directly.

This transformation became the greatest challenge to the feudal elites of the Asian states. When they came under direct or indirect colonial rule, they saw that their own traders could acquire new sources of influence and power. In the Malay archipelago, Bugis and Minangkabau businessmen joined Chinese, Arab and Indian merchants in seeking out foreign officials and trading organisations to bypass the traditional ruling class. The threat of being displaced by newly enriched elites had become real. Some members of the ruling elite found safety by becoming colonial bureaucrats; others turned to anti-colonial nationalism to win back their pride and self-respect. Malay aristocrats trained for the civil service, while their military counterparts in Thailand evolved a nationalist ethos. In Dutch-controlled lands, Sukarno and Mohammed Hatta thought their people needed higher ideals than commercial wealth. But, whichever route they took, they sought out allies among those who had mastered the skills to exploit the larger and more open trading world.[10]

During the last century of the millennium, global economics vied with political power, for the first time in history, to play the dominant role in our lives. This phenomenon was most strikingly obvious in maritime countries like Japan and its former colonies of Taiwan and (South) Korea and the new nations created out of the Malay archipelago. Japan, and then Hong Kong, Singapore, Malaysia and the Philippines have been exposed to the two largest trading empires created by sea power during the past two centuries, the highly structured empire of the British and the informal one of their successors, the Americans.[11] The impact of such changes has now brought the possibility that the global markets that grew so spectacularly in recent decades will finally triumph over residual feudal and authoritarian structures.

For Asia, especially Southeast Asia where trade had been more open and flexibly managed for centuries, the new millennium offers its greatest challenge, and opportunity. Will the new nation-states allow their nationalism to turn them back to older value-systems and keep their entrepreneurs out of political power, or will they allow power to be shared and accept that their new merchant classes offer the best chance for their countries to thrive in an increasingly borderless economic order? Whichever the outcome, the choice itself highlights a fundamental economic power shift during the past millennium that no state can afford to underestimate.

Notes

1. David W. Rudner. 1994. *Caste and Capitalism in Colonial India: The Nattukottai Chettiars.* Berkeley: University of California Press, chaps. 2 and 3, pp. 15-50; Wang Gungwu. 1989. *The Culture of Chinese Merchants,* Toronto & York University Joint Centre for Asia Pacific Studies (Working Paper Series No. 57), Toronto.

2. J.C. van Leur. 1955. *Indonesian Trade and Society: Essays in Asian Social and Economic History.* Translated by James S. Holmes and A. van Marle. the Hague: van Hoeve; Lawrence P. Briggs. 1951. *The Ancient Khmer Empire.* Philadelphia: American Philosophical Society; Jacques Dumarcay. 1985. *Borobodur.* Edited and Translated by Michael Smithies. Singapore: Oxford University Press; Henri Stierlin. 1984. *The Cultural History of Angkor.* London: Aurum Press.

3. F.Hirth and W.W. Rockhill. 1911. *Chau Ju-Kua: His work on the Chinese and Arab Trade in the Twelfth and Thirteenth Centuries, Entitled Chu-fan-chi.* Translated from the Chinese, and annotated by Frederich Hirth and W.W. Rockhill. St. Petersburg: Imperial Academy of Science; Ibn Batuta. 1983. *Travels in Asia and Africa, 1325–1354.* London: Routledge and Kegan Paul (Reprint of first edition published in 1929).

4. Wang Gungwu. 1998. *The Nanhai Trade: The Early History of Chinese Trade in the South China Sea.* Second edition. Singapore: Times Academic Press; Edward H. Schafer. 1954. *The Empire of Min.* Rutland, VT: C.E. Tuttle; O.W. Wolters. 1967. *Early Indonesian Commerce: A Study of the Origins of Srivijaya.* Ithaca, N.Y.: Cornell University; Hirth and Rockhill. 1911. *Chau Ju-kua* (see note 3).

5. Roderich Ptak and Dietmar Rothermund. Eds. 1991. *Emporia, Commodities and Entrepreneurs in Asian Maritime Trade.* Stuttgart: Franz Steiner Verlag; Om Prakash. 1997. *European Commercial Expansion in Early Modern Asia.* Aldershot, Hants.: Variorum.

6. Wang Gungwu. 1998. "Ming foreign relations: Southeast Asia". In *The Cambridge History of China, vol. 8: The Ming Dynasty, 1368–1644, Part 2,*

edited by Denis Twitchett and Frederick W. Mote. Cambridge and New York: Cambridge University Press, pp. 301–332, and 992–995; Louise Levathes. 1994. *When China Ruled the Seas: The Treasure Fleet of the Dragon Throne, 1405–1433*. New York: Simon & Schuster.

7. M.A.P. Meilink-Roelofsz. 1962. *Asian Trade and European Influence in the Indonesian Archipelago between 1500 and about 1630*. The Hague: Nijhoff; William L. Schurz. 1959. *The Manila Galleon*. New York: Dutton (reprint of 1939 edition); Kristof Glamann. 1958. *Dutch-Asiatic Trade, 1620–1740*. Copenhagen/The Hague: Danish Science Press and the Martinus Nijhoff; John E. Wills, Jr. 1974. *Pepper, Guns and Parleys: The Dutch East India Company and China, 1622/1662–1681*. Cambridge, Mass.: Harvard University Press; and John E. Wills, Jr. 1984. *Embassies and Illusions: Dutch and Portuguese Envoys to Kang-hsi, 1666–1687*. Cambridge, Mass.: East Asian Monographs, Harvard University.

Chinese Values and Memories of Modern War[*]

I am greatly honoured by the invitation to give this year's Sir
Edward 'Weary' Dunlop AsiaLink Lecture. In his Inaugural Lecture
in 1993, the former prime minister Paul Keating said he believed
that the life of Weary Dunlop should be required reading for every
young Australian. I agree with that judgment. One of the reasons
Mr Keating gave for this struck the strongest chord with me. Let
me quote what he said, "He (that is, Weary Dunlop) embraced
change, he encouraged it, he believed in the possible — for all
his love of Australia, he imagined a *different* Australia". Those are
very stirring words in honour of an extraordinary Australian, indeed
a remarkable human being.

It may seem odd that I should lead from Weary Dunlop's
memories of war to reflect on Asian, and specially Chinese, values
here. His record of war experiences is extraordinary and no
equivalent can be found in Asia. The debate about Asian values
is also extraordinary, especially when, as I shall show later, it is
really about China. What I hope to do is to use the contrasts

---

[*]This is the revised version of the Dunlop AsiaLink Lecture which I gave in
Melbourne on 17 December 1998.

between Western and Chinese memories of war in order to argue that, despite the political hijacking of the subject of Asian values, cultural differences are deep and persistent, and should not be allowed to be so politicised, or trivialised by political agendas.

Let me begin with Weary Dunlop's record of the war.[1] I first heard of him from friends who had been beneficiaries of the Colombo Plan and had known him as the President of the Victorian branch of the Australian-Asian Association. Also, his efforts to establish friendships with the Japanese whose war-time behaviour he deeply hated had made him into a legendary figure in his own lifetime. But it was not until his War Diaries were published that the world came to know the extent of his heroism and the depth of his magnanimity. I was in Hong Kong when Weary Dunlop died in 1993, and was still there when Sue Ebury's biography appeared.[2] A number of my Australian, and especially my medical, colleagues had known him and commented on the fact that, at last, we had a full account of what he had devoted his life to doing after the war.

In Weary Dunlop's Diaries, I noticed his amazing ability to capture the details of everything he experienced and thought worth noting. His powers of observation in the midst of turmoil and threats were particularly impressive. For example, when he was moved out of Bandung on the way to the Malay peninsula and eventually to the Burma-Thailand railway, he describes the journey down to the plains of Batavia (now Jakarta), "It was a magnificent sight to see the green jungle valleys full of mist and the verdant mountain tops striking up on all sides, as the train wove a tortuous course amongst them. Java is almost terrifyingly green and verdant (a green succulent death) ..." (p. 130). And he has other similar observations about Malayan peoples and Thai landscapes. In the heart of the soldier-surgeon were the sensibilities of a poet. I am reminded of the many poets that modern wars had spawned in British tradition, and now also in the Australian tradition. Weary Dunlop's poetry took a different form.

Another revealing passage is, "Somehow, peace has been spoiled for me: I crave movement, adventure, new countries, variety — the strangeness of things, and shun the old life of solid endeavour amongst people who haven't suffered or been unsettled." (p. 136) Yet Weary Dunlop did return to a life of solid endeavour, one that was dedicated to those who needed medical attention, and looked to an Australia that would play a totally new role in Asia.

What Weary Dunlop and his fellow prisoners endured to build the railway between Thailand and Burma is now better known, but his unique record of how a modern-trained surgeon adapted to jungle diseases and innovated with the minimum of medicines and equipment remains a magnificent example of strength and courage. I don't think I need to remind you of the careful descriptions he made of what had to be done at the camps at Kintok Mountain, at Tarsau and at Chungkai during the worst year, that of 1943.

I shall not emphasise so much his personal distinction as what he stood for. I believe that he stood for a set of values that was the product of the history and culture of the British people who came to settle in Australia, and that in turn marked some of the best qualities of European civilisation. When I stress this part of him, I do not underestimate the influence of the Australian experience on those values. What I wish to do is to relate the values to those that Australia has encountered in the Asia-Pacific region, and share my thoughts about certain questions about such values today.

Perhaps the best way to begin is quote from the Foreword to Weary Dunlop's War Diaries by Colonel Sir Laurens van der Post. He said,

> "... there is something instinctively humiliating about
> giving up the battle and letting oneself be incarcerated
> in apparent safety while one's countrymen and allies

lay down their lives in hundreds of thousands. In
Europe, as far as military prisoners of war were concerned, this instinctive reaction was mitigated by the
fact that prisoners of war were not dishonoured in the
code of their captors, and allowed certain minimums
of decency and self respect. In the Far East, ... it was
a totally different story. This feeling of humiliation ...
was heightened to an almost unbearable degree by the
contempt in which the Japanese held all prisoners of
war. It was a contempt that one could not ignore and
dismiss merely as an archaic prejudice of a mediaeval
elite, because the Japanese themselves practised what
they preached and died ... rather than submit to what
they regarded as the ultimate degradation of surrender."

The larger issue, of course, is not only about surrender and
prisoners of war. It covers the total experience of war in the
respective countries in Europe and eastern Asia, including the
memories of war and the cultural attitudes which such memories
convey. Although the quote from Laurens van der Post refers to
the different value system of the Japanese in war, the even more
different traditions of China should remind us that the Asian
values debate of recent years is not simply one between politicians
and journalists, but reflects genuine differences which do need to
be treated sensitively.

I shall lead into the debate by comparing Weary Dunlop's
response, as an example of Western attitudes to war, with those
of his Asian contemporaries in the region. I was reminded of this
recently when various countries either celebrated or did not
celebrate the 50th anniversary of the end of the Second World
War, or the Pacific War.[3]

As you know, the end of that war was followed by a large
number of histories and memoirs by the protagonists, especially

the victors. There were also innumerable novels and films, paintings and photographs to commemorate the heroism of the soldiers and the courage displayed by the victims of war. In time, there were also many depictions of the cowardly and the greedy, the innocent and the guilty. The whole gamut of experience and emotion was recorded in one form or another.

The distribution of such works was uneven. In general, the English-speaking world dominated, with works in French and other European languages making important contributions. Understandably, those who lived in areas where no actual battles were fought would have observed from the sidelines, with little to say. But even in the countries that provided the battlefields, non-combatants had little to contribute. This was particularly true of Asia, where the major theatres of war were China and Southeast Asia, and parts of the South Pacific. The most intense fighting occurred in North and Central China, and also went on for the longest period of time, predating the beginning of the Pacific War by more than four years. Apart from that, the Burma and New Guinea campaigns lasted longest and produced the greatest number of war casualties. For most of Southeast Asia, the actual fighting was brief. War for the people there was largely a problem of grim survival and more or less painful adaptation during the Japanese occupation.

Under such circumstances, it is not surprising that memorable accounts have been limited to the European and Japanese combatants, notably in New Guinea, Burma and, at least in terms of strategic miscalculations, also British Malaya. For the rest, some personal experiences did go on record, and a few local novels and short stories were set during periods of Japanese occupation. Even among the major protagonists, the record is variable. The British, Americans and Australians produced many histories and memoirs, including official histories complete with volumes of selected documents.

As for the vanquished Japanese, they ignored the war for the two decades after their defeat. Their response was to put their heads down and concentrate on national recovery. Only when they had proved themselves in peace, with most remarkable achievements in economic growth, did they return to assess the events that led the country to the catastrophic decision to attack Pearl Harbour and conquer Southeast Asia. Once begun, however, a flood of books has appeared about the Pacific War. These have varied from defensive rationalisations that stressed Japan's having been forced to go to war, to a few fierce exposures of Japanese atrocities which the government had tried to hide. The controversies aroused over the behaviour of the Japanese armies towards non-combatants, who had been subjected to their cruelties, have opened up old wounds without satisfying the peoples who had suffered from the war, notably those in China.[4]

In Southeast Asia, there were very few attempts to write about the war, or to commemorate it in any way. The world-wide coverage of the 50th anniversary of VE day and VJ Day in 1995 produced little response in the region. Only Singapore, the Philippines and parts of Malaysia, offered official remembrance. Much of it represented memories of Japanese atrocities towards the Chinese. Where the indigenous peoples are concerned, only the Filipinos were proud of their compatriots who had fought the Japanese. I grew up in British Malaya during the war and the Japanese occupation left a deep impression on me. I know how little was written about the war. My knowledge of it came from reading the many books written by British, Australian and American participants and by a handful of locals who had stories to tell and wrote either in English or in Chinese.

I attribute the relative silence from those in Southeast Asia who had fought or suffered during the war to the fact that most of them were not protagonists. It was a war between two sets of imperialists, Japan and the colonial powers, and not their war. Therefore, they have not been keen to remember it. This was not really so for the Chinese in Southeast Asia. For most of them, the war was about China and largely an extension of the war in China. Their fears, therefore, were due more to the fact that Japan was an enemy in China than that it was an enemy of the West. It was a terror that infused all aspects of their memories of the occupation, including the memory of those people involved in the China Relief Fund who had worked hard and systematically since 1937 to collect funds for China. For them, Japanese atrocities had already occurred in China. Images of those atrocities were vivid in their minds long before the Japanese arrived. Furthermore, many Chinese had come from China since 1937, some with personal memories of what the Japanese had done. Certainly, all Chinese were fully aware of Japanese atrocities in Nanjing and elsewhere.

They thus experienced all kinds of fear during the Japanese Occupation. Possibly the greatest fear was that of being accused of collaboration with the Japanese. This fear was greater than that of being exposed as being anti-Japanese. There were many anti-Japanese groups among the Chinese. We tend to remember those similar to the Malayan Communist Party (the MCP), or the MCP component of the Malayan Peoples' Anti-Japanese Army (the MPAJA), but not all anti-Japanese movements were communist. Many were simply nationalists. These included members of the Kuomintang, and others who were anti-Japanese before 1941. Many of them were also killed in the towns while others fought in the jungle.

What most Chinese felt about the invading Japanese was very much heightened by what was happening in China. They remembered only too well what their relatives in China had told them. It did not have to be north-central China where the Japanese had been specially ferocious. Provinces like Fujian and Guangdong, from where most Chinese and their descendants originated, had not seen a great deal of fighting, but the stories of deprivation, cruelty and fear were no less dramatic and memorable. The pervasive sense of Chinese nationalism was in many ways more intense outside China, because it had been highlighted by a more sophisticated and accessible mass media. Compared to people living in small villages in China who might not have known too much about what was happening in the rest of the country, and there were many parts of China where villagers had no experience of war at all, the Chinese in Southeast Asia had a much more vivid picture of the Sino-Japanese war through a relatively efficient Chinese news network. The kind of information available to them formed an important background to who remembers, why they remember, and what they select to remember afterwards.

Yet the Chinese left no significant writings about the war. The only exceptions were those of Tan Kah Kee and Chin Kee Onn.[5] There was also the volume listing the victims of Japanese killings in Singapore and Malaysia, which was used to persuade the Japanese government to admit guilt and compensate the families of the victims.[6] But there was nothing like the outpourings from the European protagonists in the war. One explanation was that the Chinese were preoccupied with what was happening in China, with the civil war during the period 1945–1949. But, soon after the victory of the People's Liberation Army over the Nationalist forces in 1949, a new interest in military achievements appeared. Events on the Korean peninsula and then the Cold War between the United States and the Soviet Union, however, overshadowed the older story of the Sino-Japanese war. In China, it was not until the 1990s that serious histories about the Sino-Japanese War began to be written.[7]

Another explanation was that the Chinese in Southeast Asia had to struggle hard merely to survive after the end of the war;

they had to re-orient themselves to local nationalisms and the growing international ideology of communism. The few published writings by Chinese in Malaya seemed to have lost meaning and relevance as the struggle with the Malayan Communist Party merged into the larger success of the Chinese Communist Party on the Chinese mainland. Elsewhere, local nationalist movements dominated all developments, and the Chinese found that their bitter memories about their treatment by the Japanese were of no importance to the new governments. Those who had looked to China found that there was little interest in the past as the People's Republic urged them to concentrate on its revolutionary future. Much of the anger was focused on the corruption of the dictatorial regime of the Guomindang government, first in Nanjing and then in Taipei. In turn, the government in Taipei concentrated its fire on the evils of communism. Actual memories of the Sino-Japanese War were allowed to languish and fade. The moral judgments about the war by victims on the periphery could easily be relegated to mere personal resentments and anecdotal memories that could be expected soon to fade. The respective governments used anti-Japan memories mainly as a political weapon to be wielded when it suited national interests.

However, the factors mentioned above do not adequately explain the behaviour of the Chinese, especially those in China. Compared with the range of writings by the Europeans about the war in Europe, the Chinese really wrote very little about the war in China. There was nothing like the war diaries of men like Weary Dunlop or the war memoirs of military leaders. Why did they not write more?

This difference leads me to the larger debate about Asian values today. Let me outline the key features of the debate which show how the so-called Asian values are really those Confucian Chinese values that seem to oppose what have been called Western values.

This is a curious debate which gained prominence only after the end of the Cold War. It was as if, with the end of the ideological struggle between capitalism and communism, there was a political vacuum that had to be filled. Certainly, when the issue of culture arose to replace ideology, political leaders, commentators and journalists were quick to pounce on it. The subject has had wider ramifications than anyone expected, and the focus has shifted many times. Two features are specially relevant here because they both revolve round questions pertaining to China. Let me quickly outline the background.

The really odd thing is that Singapore bore the brunt of the attack on Asian values.[8] The matter had begun very modestly in the early 1980s with the call to introduce a course on Confucian ethics in Singapore secondary schools to accompany courses on ethics each within the framework of religions like Christianity, Islam, Buddhism and Hinduism. This was criticised first on the grounds that Confucianism was not a religion but more like a state ideology. Given the earlier campaign to encourage Mandarin speaking among the ethnic Chinese in Singapore, the new move seemed like something that could lead to too great a dominance of Chinese culture in a multi-ethnic society. The more serious attack accused the government of using Confucianism to justify its authoritarian rule. This became more prominent when Deng Xiaoping's reforms in China turned out to be extraordinarily successful. This success was in such sharp contrast to Gorbachev's efforts to introduce liberal political reforms in the Soviet Union that it gained world attention. Thus, when Deng Xiaoping showed his approval of Singapore's achievements, this was not only a boost to the status of Singapore's leaders, but also a red flag to those who saw a Chinese communist regime supporting another authoritarian Chinese polity.

In this way, a local issue of education and culture was raised to the international stage. What had begun as defence against detribalisation, an attempt at reculturation of young Singaporeans, became an object of fierce attacks in the Western media. What was emphasised instead was the apparent underlying political agenda, what was seen as the neutralising of dissent and opposition. The attacks came not only from the liberal core of the West but also from former enthusiasts for the People's Republic who were disillusioned with Mao Zedong's revolution and who thought Deng Xiaoping had betrayed socialist ideals.

It was a very mixed bag of criticism, but each of the antogonists had a political agenda. The most consistent of them were the human rights activists who saw the issue in terms of a self-serving elite defending their illiberal and undemocratic ways. From Singapore, the defenders argued robustly that Asian values were to provide the antidote against all that was going wrong in the West, the excessive individualism, the failure of moral authority, the flabbiness in the welfare state, and so on.

The politics of the debate need not concern us here. What is of concern is that the protagonists have narrowed the debate to the politics of extreme either/or positions. On the one hand, those who have good words to say about Asian values are seen as reactionaries, elitists, undemocratic and authoritarian types, who are trying to rationalise themselves out of the issue of universal human rights. On the other hand, those who mock the espousals of Asian values have been described as slavishly pro-Western and dangerous populists, potentially rebels and anarchists who are ultimately willing to support Western dominance of the world. These positions have tended to divert the debate from the question of what cultural values mean and trivialise legitimate efforts to point to genuine and significant differences between peoples and cultures.

There is now a tendency to assume that political protagonists speak for the religious and philosophical ideas that lie behind the debate. On the one hand, there are scholars who write at length to show how some political leaders have misquoted Confucius for their own ends. And there are also those who write to support the way some traditional values have been selectively picked by political leaders to bolster their cause. On the other hand, Western political leaders and the media have used the debate to determine which Asian leaders are liberal and democratic and which authoritarian according to their cultural orientation.

This becomes even more interesting when it becomes clear that the Asian values debate in the minds of many political leaders is really about Chinese values. It has nothing to do with Japan, hence I do not include any comparisons with the Japanese here. The debate had begun as Confucian ethics in Singapore. This was reinforced by the East Asian miracle of Japan and the Newly Industrialising Economies of South Korea, Taiwan, Hong Kong and Singapore, the so-called four Tigers, especially when it was concluded that the secret of their success lay in Confucianism, the only factor that was common to all five territories. Thus there was praise and wonder at the value of that ancient body of ethical discipline. But a series of events followed which turned the tide. China after 1978 began its Long March to hyper-growth in the 1980s, but this ended with the tragedy of Tiananmen in 1989. When the Soviet Union collapsed soon afterwards and Cold War ideology became meaningless, Confucianism quickly became the short-hand for Chinese power and ambition. For example, Chinese overseas seen as both Confucian and capitalist, who were accredited with helping the People's Republic in its economic reforms, began to be portrayed as a potential force for Chinese aggrandisement. This is a curious throwback to the language of the Cold War as applied to eastern Asia.

I have already mentioned how Chinese/Confucian values became part of the human rights and democracy debate. To add to the complications, the debate has also converged with the uncertainties of post-Cold War strategic thinking. Between the Western triumphalism that spoke of "the end of history", and the need to identify future threats as found in the "clash of civilisations", "Asian values" has entered the scene as a potential source of future conflict. The new premise is that, if Asian values regain credibility, the West would have to gird its loins for battle.[9]

I think I have said enough to suggest why many people see that cultural differences are themselves under threat from the political struggle going on. The dominance of international politics is obviously not new. The decades of the Cold War had done much to diminish cultural values in the name of the dichotomy of capitalism and communism. What we face is another attempt to place the world in an either/or, black and white, situation. "Asian values" is in danger of becoming an abstract code phrase replacing that of the more physically powerful "evil empire". In this context, it is not surprising to find that, when the world's only superpower is scouring the horizon for the next challenge to its supremacy, the only possible candidate is China. When put in military terms, the question of attitudes to war becomes significant. This brings me back to Weary Dunlop and memories of war.

It has been noted how Weary Dunlop suffered in Japanese concentration camps and forgave his jailers after the war. I am reminded of the proverb he is known to have quoted, "all men are equal in the face of suffering and death", which allowed him to befriend various Japanese leaders in pursuit of a new basis for good Australia-Japan relations. I am not sure if Japanese military figures believed in that proverb. Certainly the Chinese had distinctively different views about what to remember about war, what should be recorded, and what values should influence moral judgments about war.

It should not surprise us that there is nothing in China remotely like Weary Dunlop's war diaries. They are unusual even in Europe and America. But they are consistent with the Western value system which recognises that war is a normal condition that we have to learn to live with. As Clausewitz puts it, "war is a political instrument, a continuation of political relations, a carrying out of the same by other means". Its consequences may be simultaneously tragic and heroic. Readiness to defend one's country, personal courage in battle, and remembrance of those who died in war, are values that are highly regarded. There is, therefore, a distinguished tradition of memoirs and military epics and histories whose earliest forms can be traced back to Homer's Iliad and Thucydides' history of the Peloponnesian war. This tradition was further developed by Roman rulers and politicians like Julius Caesar and Tacitus and by historians like Josephus. Later, there were great records of war written by clerics and churchmen, for example, those of the Crusades and the remarkable accounts of the conquest of New Spain in the New World. In modern times, this had been given greater blessing by nation-states in which the citizenry proved their solidarity through nationalism and their memories of war became vital parts of the cultural heritage.

Again and again, war was described in terms of heroism, and the narratives brought out the personal achievements of friend and foe. In time, feudal and knightly standards of behaviour led to codes of conduct that now guide modern wars, including the treatment of the dead and wounded and those captured in war. With the modern empires, official war histories, memoirs of generals and other officers, regimental histories, personal diaries and letters all contributed to a keen sense of military exploits on behalf of one's country. There is nothing anywhere to compare with the hundreds of thousands of volumes the Americans have accumulated about their Civil War. I also recall being very struck when I came to Australia to find that the only national museum in Canberra at that time was the War Memorial. One of the most memorable seminars I attended during my years at the ANU, was one by Ken Inglis comparing the various war memorials around the country.[10] Although these were not to celebrate war but rather the fortitude and heroism of people who had to face and deal with war, they still surprised me. There was nothing in my Chinese background, or in my study of Chinese history, to prepare me for the intensity and pride which accompanied these monuments to war memories.

The contrast with why and how the Chinese remembered their wars is great. Chinese history is littered with wars, great and small, and with innumerable rebellions. War was important to rulers. All the dynasties were founded through war. Their earliest records, whether cut into the so-called oracle bones of the 2nd millennium, B.C. or inscribed on bamboo slips in China's first books, often recorded victories and defeats in war. Certainly the victories were celebrated and immortalised by rulers rather like the friezes and cuneiform records of the Babylonian empire, or some of the striking accounts in the Old Testament. But the more extended Chinese records about war were official reports about triumphs or disasters. During the so-called "feudal" (*fengjian*) period of China's own period of warring states during the 1st millennium, B.C., there were chronicles about war, diplomacy and governance. Even when Confucius compiled the Spring and Autumn Annals for the 7th and 6th centuries B.C., much of the annals referred to victories and defeat in war. But these records were official ones, and none of them described any personal heroism or showed the feelings or private faces of the protagonists.

The great Han dynasty historian, Sima Qian, has sometimes been compared to Thucydides, but he was no military historian.

His emphasis was on governance, and war was but a necessary and technical part of that governance. When his work became the model of all official dynastic histories thereafter, it put war records in their place as routine accounts of one of the unenviable tasks of officialdom. In these official histories, there were biographies that heaped praise and registered rewards for loyal commanders who won, and approved the punishment of those who lost, but those on heroic military men were few and far between. Documents by individual mandarins about the progress of military expeditions do exist, but they were written as reports to be used for the official records.

The remarkable exploits by patriotic Chinese who defended the frontiers, or fought in rebellions against corrupt and tyrannical rule, did survive in popular stories, including the exceptional story of Hua Mulan, the woman warrior, which has become a successful Walt Disney film shown around the world. However, it was not until the 12th century that these stories, first strung together by professional storytellers, were written down. After the 15th century, some were to become classic fiction, like the *Three Kingdoms* (San Guo), *The Water-Margin*, also known in translation as *All Men are Brothers* (Shuihu Zhuan). They were so successful that they spawned two kinds of romances that have entertained the Chinese ever since: the genres of popular historical fiction and that of "armed knights" (*wuxia*) novels. They are both still being written and are widely read. Some have been translated into several languages and made into feature and television films. What made them popular was the emphasis on martial skills, survival strategies, personal relations and self-discovery, and of course, good entertaining writing. But, they have as little relevance to war histories as films like *High Noon* and other Hollywood Westerns have to histories of the American Civil War.

This is not to say that the Chinese did not think deeply about war. We all know that Sun Zi's Treatise on War is full of axioms about preparations for war, strategms to ensure victory, and why war should be avoided if at all possible. This classic, now augmented by new discoveries of another text, has been the standby of every general in Chinese history. This work was even more greatly prized when, in more recent dynasties, the literati mandarins were also expected to conduct military operations. They were not trained in military academies and had to resort to that text as their main standby on how to conduct wars. The point is that the business of war was always a matter for the emperors, who increasingly expected their senior civilian officials to direct them. With such a heritage, China simply could not have produced a Homer or a Thucydides. Outside the chronicles, we can find fragments of anecdotal material about the personality of some generals and the outcome of some campaigns. But very early on, at the beginning of the 2nd century, B.C., the commanders who helped found the new Han dynasty were seen as threats and the emperor found excuses to have them all removed, if not executed. The status of soldiers was equated to loyal armed peasants who provided military fodder when armies had to be raised.

By the Tang dynasty (7th–10th centuries), the power of the new "aristocratic" military was systematically curbed. Throughout the Song dynasty (10th–13th centuries), civilian mandarins were expected to command the expeditionary armies. While the soldiers still did the actual fighting, the mandarins were expected to do the strategic thinking. And, of course, they wrote the reports. They reported according to the standard form and in elegant officialese, strictly in conformity with the orthodox interpretations of Confucian values. The conventional way was to say that the victories came from the emperor's virtue as recognised by Heaven and his successful policies were implemented by loyal mandarins and officers, while the defeats were invariably due to poor commanders and unruly troops. It was a convention that did not inspire much courage and heroism in battle, but it did give the mandarins the power to keep the generals and soldiers in their place.

These values affected even the military conquests by the non-Chinese Mongols who established the Yuan dynasty (13th to 14th centuries) as well as the warrior founders of the Manchu Qing dynasty (17th to 20th centuries). The official histories that were eventually compiled in Chinese could, in no way, capture the martial spirit and splendid formations of these tribal soldiers on horseback. To grasp the magnitude of their great military achievements, we would have to look at the Mongol epics, widely read also in Persian, Arabic and Turkic languages, and at the earlier Manchu records of the 17th century which, though less elegiac than those in Mongol, did try to convey the splendours of conquest. After the 18th century, however, the Manchu were sufficiently sinicised to adopt Confucian formulations and bureaucratise their military histories. The deep-rooted Chinese value system had won out.

I have said enough to show how a different tradition concerning the status of soldiers produced different values about war. It may be argued that China's tradition did not come from modern warfare, and should not be compared with what modern nations like America and Australia do. That is quite right, but a value system does not change easily once firmly established for hundreds if not thousands of years. When we come down to modern times, what do we find? Let us not take the disastrous wars of the 19th century which the Chinese fought (often fought under the once heroic warrior officers of Manchu or Mongol origins) against the British and the French in traditional ways. By the 20th century, Chinese armies were fighting with modern equipment and had often been trained by European officers. Many of their officers were trained in Europe or America. Of course, their main enemies were either other Chinese armies in a long-drawn civil war, or the Japanese, who had their own unique traditions, as mentioned by Laurens van der Post. However, as the lack of writings immediately after the Second World War and other Chinese wars show, there was little basic change in their attitudes to war or in the way they chose to remember the wars themselves.

Although the Chinese military today on both sides of the Taiwan Straits are modernising fast, it is perhaps too early to look for behaviour, style and practices associated with histories and memories of war that are similar to those of modern armies in the West. For one thing, it would be true to say that the Chinese had too many defeats and not enough victories to write about. It is nevertheless interesting to note that the Chinese have accounts of executions and atrocities by the enemy, but none by, or of, prisoners of war. A few histories of various campaigns have recently appeared but there has not been the tradition of official war histories or documentary collections. As for biographies, there are now brief lives of generals, and some military men have told their own stories, notably in the monthly *Biographical Literature* and other popular magazines, but there are as yet no war memorials, or days of commemoration, no detailed war diaries or full-length memoirs. The Chinese had fought a most bitter civil war, but neither the victors nor the losers have offered anything remotely comparable to those accounts available of the English Civil War, the Hundred Years War, the Scottish Highlands War, least of all the American Civil War, just to mention those I am more familiar with. Nor, from what is known of the archives, and of the People's Liberation Army and Guomindang military historians, and of the Chinese tradition they have inherited, can we expect them to produce comparable records for some time.

Of course, one may ask, why should they? And that is the point I wish to make here. Modernisation may mean that armies learn the same tactics, use the same equipment, organise the same military units to march, sing, train and fight in similar ways. But it need not necessarily mean that there will be concomitant changes in attitudes towards soldiers and war, to the way political power is shared, or to the mindset about the proper role of government and defence policy-making. For the Chinese who have inherited an imperial tradition and imperial borders, and are still struggling to transform themselves into a nation-state, it may take even longer.

Weary Dunlop would, I am sure, prefer that there be no fighting at all. His war experiences and his life work taught him to respect the cultural values of others. The fact that the Chinese do not commemorate wars the way that Western peoples do may tell us something about values that is more serious and enduring than the current political debate about Asian values. It reminds us to resist simplifying cultural issues in black and white dichotomous ways. Understanding cultural difference is hard work. Let us not allow impatient and lazy minds in search of slogans and sound bytes to rush us into judgment about what values should or should not stand in the way of universalist progress.

Notes

1. E. E. Dunlop. *The War Diaries of Weary Dunlop: Java and the Burma-Thailand Railway, 1942–1945.* Melbourne: Penguin, 1990.

2. Sue Ebury. *Weary: The Life of Sir Edward Dunlop.* Ringwood, Vic. Australia: Viking, 1944.

3. A recent example from the same war region is P. Lim Pui Huen and

Diana Wong, eds. *War and Memory in Malaysia and Singapore*. Singapore: Institute of Southeast Asian Studies, 2000.

4. George Hicks. *Japan's War Memories: Amnesia or Concealment?* Aldershot, England: Ashgate, 1997.

5. Tan Kah Kee (Chen Jiageng). *Nanqiao huiyilu* (Memoirs of a Nanyang Chinese). In two volumes. Singapore, 1946. (Several editions published in Hong Kong, Taipei, Shanghai, and Beijing.) The English edition is *The Memoirs of Tan Kah Kee*. Edited and translated with notes by A.H.C. Ward, Raymond W. Chu and Janet Salaff. Singapore: Singapore University Press, 1994. Chin Kee Onn's early work is *Malaysia Upside Down*. Singapore. Printed by Jitts. 1946.

6. *Dazhan yu Nanqiao: Malaiya zhi bu* (The War and the Nanyang Chinese: Malaya). Singapore , 1947. Also, Hsu Yun-ts'iao, edited by Cai Shijun. *Xin Ma huaren kang Ri shiliao, 1937–1945*. (Anti-Japanese activities of the Malayan and Singapore Chinese: Historical documents, 1937–1945). Singapore: Wen-shi publishers, 1984; Su Yunfeng. *Xin Ma huaren zai kang Ri zhanzheng zhong di xisheng yu fengxian, 1937–1945*. (Sacrifices and Contributions of the Malayan and Singapore Chinese during the war against Japan, 1937–1945). Hong Kong: Dangdai Yazhou yanjiu zhongxin, 1987.

7. The issue of *Jindaishi yanjiu* (Journal of Modern History), no. 113, of September 1999, celebrating the 50th Anniversary of the People's Republic of China, was dedicated to surveys of the historical writings produced from 1949 to 1999. The chapter on military history was written by Mao Haijian and Liu Tong, pp. 117–130. The authors examine the collections of documents pertaining to various wars and campaigns produced during the 1950s and compared them with the vast amount of materials published in the 1980s and 1990s, including a new series of biographies of the great marshals who had fought in the Sino-Japanese War and a small number of their memoirs.

8. The beginnings are traced in Tu Wei-ming, *Confucian Ethics Today; the Singapore Challenge*. Singapore: Curriculum Development Institute of Singapore and Federal Publications, 1984. For a recent survey of the issues

by a panel on "Asian Values: Asian Miracle or Asian Mirage?", see Ooi Giok Ling and R.S. Rajan. Eds. *Singapore: The Year in Review, 1998.* Singapore: The Institute of Policy Studies and Times Academic Press, 1999, pp. 102–135.

9. Wang Gungwu, "A Machiavelli for Our Times: Huntington's Clash of Civilizations: II", *The National Interest*, no. 46, Winter 1996/97, pp. 69–73.

10. Kenneth S. Inglis. *Anzac Remembered: Selected Writings by K.S. Inglis.* Chosen and edited by John Lack, with an introduction by Jay Winter. Parkville, Vic.: History Monographs Series, no. 23, University of Melbourne, 1998.

Modern Work Cultures and the Chinese*

I am greatly honoured by the invitation to speak at this Commonwealth Forum on Open Learning. It is remarkable how quickly continuing education or distance learning has been extended around the Commonwealth. This most innovative approach to education is of growing importance and the work of the Commonwealth of Learning is a considerable inspiration. The theme of the conference, "Empowerment through Knowledge and Technology" reminds us that the demand for education continues to expand and career-oriented knowledge is increasingly dependent on mastering new skills. This has led me to focus on the topic of work cultures. We are all living longer, changing technologies are very demanding, and we are beginning to see how this perspective of the future affects our attitudes to work. It has even been suggested that regular secure jobs may soon be a thing of the past. Fortunately, there has been much improvement in methods of delivery to bring a greater variety of education and

---

*This is a revised version of the Asa Briggs Lecture given at the Pan Commonwealth Forum on Open Learning held in Brunei Daressalam in 1999. The lecture was delivered on 2 March 1999.

training to all who need it. This may better prepare us for the day when each of us will need many skills to keep working.

We have high ideals for education as the key to the transmission of knowledge and values as well as the way to stimulate the creative imagination. But it cannot be denied that schools, colleges and universities, especially in Asia and the developing world in general, are primarily expected to get the young ready for work. Thus, while we may argue that education better prepares us for work than mere training, we still need to convince parents and students that this has practical advantages for employment. Over the past two centuries, jobs have evolved to favour increasingly those educated to think critically, those who know how to learn. With each generation, such workers are more likely to adapt to our knowledge-driven society than those trained to execute specific skills. In this context, education is not confined to enabling people with different cultural heritages to understand each other, or to help bring together the universal and perennial that each culture has to offer. It would include other features which dominate people's lives, not least the culture of work itself. I propose to talk today about this aspect of culture, that is, how people cope with changes in work cultures and what that might tell us. For this purpose, I shall take the example of China because I wish to offer a perspective on how a vast agrarian society adapts to modern work conditions. While much of that experience points to the limits of education, it also suggests that changing attitudes towards work must depend on some kind of empowerment of those being educated, as indicated in the theme of the conference.

It is appropriate that the lecture is named after Asa Briggs. His contributions to our understanding of the changing nature of work, and its impact on those who work, during the past two centuries are well known.[1] How he has related that to the way communication methods have been revolutionised has been an eye-opener to everyone. But most of all, he is an historian who loves, in his own words, history as a "serious pursuit" but also recognises "the contradictions of progress" in history, something the history of modern China had a lot of. Changes in the culture of work are no less serious and contradictory in Asia, not least in the example of the hundreds of millions of Chinese peasants adapting to a cultural revolution in the world of work. For a major transformation in work culture, England of the industrial revolution took the lead. It showed the way educational change played its part in helping people respond to the industrial revolution. China, on the other hand, with the largest peasant population in the world at the turn of this century, suffered massive shocks to its system. Its people experienced the most radical changes to their work cultures that anyone has ever endured. How they overcame such changes, how the work cultures were bridged, have lessons for the rest of us.

Before I turn to the cultures of work, let me briefly outline what education has meant for the bridging of cultures as it is more conventionally understood. In many ways, the role of education in transmitting cultural values between generations and in culture-contacts has been taken for granted. Therefore, it is easy to forget that these values include changing attitudes towards work. Education has normally functioned in the larger context in which work cultures are but a part. We all acknowledge that the transmission and enrichment of cultural values in general have always been matters of concern. In recent decades, however, responding to a rapidly changing world, to a globalizing world in which local cultural differences seem less important, there has been growing emphasis on education as the teaching and learning of scientific and technical skills. This is particularly true of developing countries which felt that they had fallen behind in these areas and must speed up the process of learning new and vital skills. All you have to do is to look at the number of schools, colleges and universities all over Asia which have greatly expanded their courses on science and technology, and the number of new institutions largely dedicated to engineering and business, to see the contrast with the more traditional institutions of the Western world.

This is understandable. As for open learning, this has been broader in conception from the start, but there is pressure on it as well to contribute directly to the acquisition of skills favoured in modern careers. In particular, the technology available for distance learning and the teaching of large numbers of students makes it easy to communicate skills which are universally valued and cut across parochial and national cultures. Where the more conventional ideas of culture are concerned, as represented in the arts and humanities, the adjustments have been more difficult and less appreciated. The transmission of such cultural values simply cannot compare with the relative ease experienced in the transfer of skills in technology and business.

Indeed, modern education of this latter kind is so successful that it will not be long before many traditional cultural values will be treated as irrelevant for most of the important linkages in the world. The growing number of people who speak the international languages of science and business will ensure that, at one level, there is immediate communication all round. Hopefully, there will always be the few in every society who specialise in the study of specific cultures and help distinctive cultures in the world to survive. If not, these cultures and their value-systems will in time disappear, in the same way that hundreds of languages, customs, artifacts and technologies have been eliminated during the past two centuries. This is, of course, a rather grim scenario. The outcome is still uncertain and may not be that bad. But the fact that many smaller cultures have disappeared is incontrovertible.

This does not have to be so for those which remain viable today. The rich variety of cultures that human beings have developed during the past five to ten millennia is a great gift from the human past. There is a store of experience and wisdom there that could be tapped for what they might be able to tell us about how to face the future, not least the place of knowledge and technology in their work cultures. It would be a tragedy if what is past is forgotten, and if it were assumed that whatever is not directly useful deserves to end up in nostalgic museums for curiosity value alone.

The point is that the world is getting smaller and this is not always kind to matters pertaining to culture. Certain powerful cultures have expanded at the expense of others. For example, modern Western culture, or in some contexts, its earlier form of Judaeo-Christian culture, or in more specific circumstances, Anglo-American culture, has expanded to many corners of the globe. Others, like Indian or Hindu-Buddhist or Sanskritic culture did have its day but are contained in a more limited area today. Similarly, East Asian, or more specifically Confucian and Taoist, culture has had considerable impact over large areas, but has been facing some very trying times since the beginning of this century. It is also readily acknowledged that Islamic culture (including its many linguistic manifestations, whether Arab, Turkic, Persian and Urdu, Bengali, Malay or Indonesian) has not stopped spreading for more than 1,300 years. Yet some of the strongest exponents of that culture have had to be very defensive in the face of globalisation pressures. As each of these historically powerful cultures expand towards one another, many cultures in between, whether local or tribal, national or mixed multicultural, have found themselves to have been under threat.

The result is that each of the now relatively few dominant cultures in the world has become both extensive and concentrated. The majority of the bearers of each of these cultures crowd closer together in larger and larger metropolises. The pressures of modern living are producing complex societies. Some cultures, such as those in modern migrant nations, e.g. United States, Canada, Mexico, Australia and Brazil, encourage the search for identity among individuals and small groups in the community. Others demand much greater conformity for nation-building purposes, and regret the variety of cultural choices that present themselves to their citizens. Yet others are themselves under threat and survive only in urban ghettos and reservations in the wilderness, and are often better represented in museums than in real life. It can even be argued that, while we may today have the illusion of great cultural wealth, many cultures are no longer independently viable and this smaller world has really made us culturally impoverished.

Of course, there are some contrary examples. In Southeast Asia, on this island of Borneo, we see the unique cultures of the Ibans and Kadazans adapting well to the pressures of modernity. What we observe is the result of good nurturing and learning, and good teaching by all means available. In this way, the more accessible cultural artifacts like their family rules and structures, their laws and customs, their manifold artistic performances, faiths and practices, texts and testimonies however transmitted, have co-mingled with the secular and efficient features of the globalizing and universal civilisation around us. Their current forms have thus provided variety and depth to the cultural heritage of Malaysia. Such examples could be an inspiration to others. Without describing it in so many words, a particular form of cultural bridging has been successfully put into practice.

I am not being sentimental about cultures which have failed altogether to preserve their distinctive features in the face of modernisation. If the bearers of these cultures are unable or unwilling to adapt to modern pressures and either choose to abandon their respective cultures, or seek to reinvent themselves in new ways, so be it. It may well be that the forces of globalisation may revive the need for people to emphasise local identities and thus give the ethnic and sub-ethnic cultures more room for refinement and preservation. I do not embrace a simple Darwinian stance on cultures. In this part of the world, I am struck by the number of minority peoples, within countries like Thailand, Myanmar and Indonesia, who have maintained their distinctive cultures in healthy condition by integrating some modern values into their own traditions. Thus they are able to strengthen their own identities in the midst of material success.

Bridging such cultures and ensuring that they are strengthened is one of the purposes of modern education. I do not know whether distance learning methods can do as well as face-to-face teaching and learning in the area of culture learning. I am impressed by what can be achieved in the area of lifelong learning where these methods have been successfully introduced. With continuing education, the bridging is helped by the maturity of the students and their ability to relate what they learn to the experiences they have had. With ever improving audio and visual aids, and the increasing range of modern communications technology, there is little doubt that knowledge gaps can be rapidly and efficiently bridged.

But we still need to be conscious of how cultural factors underlie many of the subjects we teach. For example, there is a great deal being written and taught about the work cultures embodied in modern business systems and methods. There is evidence that the advances gained through Western capitalist experiences have been absorbed in our region. Thus, local cultural values have played their part in making Chinese and Japanese entrepreneurs, for example, successful in quite different ways. In the fields of agriculture and health sciences, a bridging of cultures, one empirical and traditional and the other scientific, is occurring before our eyes. Scholars and students in Asia and in the West have much to learn from one another. They should be systematically encouraged to be aware of the cultural values involved.

Another example is our concern for the environment. There is a considerable gap in understanding here, mostly due to differences in stages of economic development and in the standards of scientific and engineering knowledge. But there are also the differences in cultural attitudes between rich and poor countries towards major kinds of pollution. The role education can play in the transmission of the latest knowledge and appreciation of environmental issues will become increasingly important. As myriads of interactions bring business systems closer together, greater attention would have to be paid not only to differences in practice and in governance and law, but also to the underlying social and cultural concerns of the people involved. The bridging of business and other work cultures is a vital part of the theme of your conference, empowerment through knowledge and technology.

This bring me to work cultures past and present. Having as background what Asa Briggs has had to say about the work revolution in Britain, I have taken my example from changes in work cultures in China. This is a subject that is relevant to the debate on how more radical changes to the nature of work may occur throughout the world in the near future, and thus how changes will be made in education to deal with them. We all know that the culture of work has changed massively in modern times. We now face the prospect that the next generation of workers may no longer need the lifelong work skills which they have been proud to master through years of apprenticeship and education. Some kinds of work will change or disappear while new kinds will be created to meet new needs. We know the broader historical trends that show the many strategies people have used to adapt to cultural change where work is concerned. I shall concentrate here on modern China, not as a country but as representing one of the largest agrarian societies in the world. It is instructive to see how its people responded to the way work cultures changed so rapidly several times during the past century.

The Chinese adapted themselves remarkably well to the traumatic changes they encountered. They endured economic disruptions, wars and civil wars, revolution in the workplace that followed alien models and then, more recently, a dismantling of structures that had shaped their work cultures for a generation. They had begun early this century with 90% of their people still tied to the land as peasants. The picture we have of them is that they eked out a living by doing their work in ways laid down by their ancestors millennia earlier. A half century later, they had become largely wage-earning in a variety of work units, cooperatives and communes created by Mao Zedong's Communist Party. These were created by the revolutionary victors acting in the name of industrial workers. Then, in another turn around led by Deng Xiaoping some twenty years ago, they confronted yet another kind of work culture that was modified from the very capitalist system that their revolution had sought to destroy.

How was this done without totally destroying the Chinese people? How have they remained so resilient and adaptable for so long and are still ready to change further? The recent history of peasant life, especially certain kinds of peasant attitudes to work, including the readiness of the ablest of them to adapt to changing conditions, may help us explain how people dealt with changes in their work cultures. They had little or no access to formal school education, but many of them showed a readiness to learn new skills under conditions of great stress. Their behaviour in meeting challenges, sometimes of desperate uncertainty, may have something to tell us about how people might approach changes in work culture. With modern education now available in so may forms, that in turn may suggest how some kinds of education can be more directly useful to cope with rapidly changing and somewhat unpredictable changes in the nature of work in the years to come.

I should emphasise that Chinese peasant life was not unique. Some aspects of the Chinese social structure, including the specific ways the peasants related to the ruling literati elites, may have made them distinct from peasantry elsewhere, but Chinese peasants shared many features common to all peasants. Also, the cliche that peasant China has been unchanging through the centuries is very misleading. Far from peasants being limited in their ability to do many kinds of work, there is ample evidence to show that Chinese peasants had always been extremely hard-headed and eclectic in their attitudes towards any kind of work that would help them make a better living. In order to do that, some may be said to have been early practitioners of lifelong learning and better adjusted in their attitudes towards re-training than those who were more formally trained and educated.

Before I deal with the transformative changes that Chinese peasants faced, let me offer you a very eloquent picture of peasants in Europe which comes remarkably close to my understanding of the way those in China made their living right up to the beginning of this century.

"The peasant survived, managed to pull through, and this was true everywhere. But it was usually thanks to plying a hundred extra trades; crafts, wine-making, haulage. We are not surprised to find the peasants of Sweden or England also working as miners, quarry men or iron workers; or the peasants of Skane becoming sailors and carrying on an active coasting trade in the Baltic or the North Sea; or that all peasants spent at least some of their time weaving, or occasionally worked as carters. When, in the late sixteenth century, a latter-day wave of serfdom descended on Istria, many of the peasants escaped to become peddlers and carriers travelling to the Adriatic ports, and some set up an elementary iron-working industry with blast furnaces in country districts ...

"In Naples, we are told there are many who do not only live by their work as day-labourers, but who every year sow six *tomola* (unit of land) of wheat or barley ... grow vegetables and take them to market, cut and sell timber and use their animals to transport goods. A recent study has also shown that they were, in addition, both borrowers and lenders of money, small-time usurers and careful herdsmen ..."

These are the words of the French historian, Fernand Braudel, taken from his book, *Civilisation and Capitalism, 15th to 18th centuries*.[2] I was struck by how well Braudel's characterisation of the European peasant describes the Chinese peasantry. Chinese peasants too were able to do a different range of tasks in order to survive, and could be said to have been equally versatile, if not more so, over the millennia.

During the 19th century, the urban pull towards industrial work began to change the peasantry in Western Europe. Asa Briggs has provided us with vivid descriptions of what happened in the cities of Victorian England.[3] His work on the Chartists and the origins of the English working-class revolt are classics. A whole generation of labour historians has been stimulated to study how people responded to new factory cultures and what this did to attitudes towards work. In more recent years, as the capitalist system adjusted to trade union power and the development of automation technologies, we now observe further changes to the nature of modern work. You all understand this because some of you have been directly involved in the restructuring of the kinds of education needed to match the changes ahead.

In China, industrialisation started late and the peasants were not forced to leave the land until the 20th century. For southern coastal China, the more adventurous among them began to do so earlier. They left China in large numbers to come to Southeast Asia or travel much further to the Americas and Australasia.[4] There they found work cultures that were totally different from what they had known at home, but they seemed to have had little difficulty adapting to different kinds of work. They simply seized what chances were made available to them and adopted different strategies to meet different conditions. For example, in colonial Southeast Asia, those who could do so moved away as soon as possible from labouring tasks to various trades. Local conditions favoured those who could turn themselves into businessmen. In the Americas, there were different patterns. While the majority stuck to the occupations in which they were tolerated, there were better educational facilities all round, and this enabled many in the second and subsequent generations to gain upward social mobility through the modern professions.

Within China, new opportunities were fewer and political conditions were chaotic for much of the first half of the 20th century. In any case, long before the peasantry was directly affected, traumatic changes in the nature of work were to hit the highly educated scholar-officials first. And these elite groups adapted badly. I am reminded of my grandfather's story. When the imperial examination system was abolished, and modern schools introduced, he and his generation who had prepared for those examinations so that they might become gentlemen and mandarins, found themselves lost. Their ruling class skills were downgraded. Many of the

older ones tried to reinvent themselves as business associates —
fixers and go-betweens for entrepreneurs. Others reemerged as
administrators and managers in larger firms. But few were successful
in their new careers. In their place was a growing class of compradores who had grown up on the China coast and learnt to
deal with the new capitalist enterprises from the West and from
Japan. They had commercial backgrounds and their education
came not from schools and books, but from practical experience.

Tertiary level education at the time did little to change
attitudes to work. Modern universities were established to help
the educated elites adapt to the new work demands. The earliest
of them had been founded by American and European missionaries
who sought to bring the latest work skills from the developed
West to a new generation of Chinese. These were followed by
some which were established by the Chinese themselves to try to
revitalise imperial Confucian values or to imitate the best examples
of what they saw in either Western or Japanese universities.[5] But
the country was in such continuous disorder that few of them
were given time and adequate support to establish a new set of
ideals that would define new standards and goals of work. The
country was simply too poor and chaotic. The universities that
were supposed to educate a new generation for the new work
culture were ill-equipped and poorly staffed. In any case, they
catered for very small numbers of elite students who had little
incentive to empathise with the bulk of the rural-based popula-
tions. External interventions, foreign threats and actual invasions,
and a series of civil wars, all conspired to make the new work
culture little understood.

Thus, for at least two generations after the fall of the Qing
empire in 1911, the old gentry or scholar-official class were still
unable to adjust. There was a refusal to change their attitude
towards unfamiliar kinds of work. They did not adjust to make

themselves available to new kinds of employers. Even those who went to modern schools could not always accept the changes. Instead, the more idealistic among them were drawn to a new activism, and turned to efforts to secure a new political and economic order which they could control. They sought to restore themselves to the positions of authority they thought were due to them as an educated elite. It led them to turn to another kind of work, that of fomenting revolution of one kind or another, and this led them to spend their lives fighting others of their kind for supremacy.

During this period of confusion, there were obvious limits to the education of the elites. For the peasantry, there was almost no education available. They were the desperate majority of the population willing to support any change that would given them the ability to respond to new work opportunities. The study by R.H. Tawney on land and labour in China in the 1920s,[6] and more recent studies of the Chinese interior provinces by Philip Huang and Ramon Myers[7] during the same period and into the 1930s, show that there were many peasants, artisans and local merchants who had also failed to adjust to the prevailing anarchy and uncertainty. What was significant were the numbers of the well-educated who could not modify their attitudes towards the changing nature of work while most of the peasantry seemed able to use their many-faceted heritage of flexible work habits to respond to the new opportunities. In short, in addition to the cultural traditions that inhibited the ruling elites, there was a growing gap in attitudes towards changing work cultures that energised the peasant majority.

Following the communist victory in 1949, the nature of work was changed decisively by decree. The political leaders brought Soviet work models to China. These revolutionaries created a totally different kind of work culture for all Chinese, an alien culture of tight social control which brought specific groups of workers together. In modified forms, this kind of worker control was extended to villages and communes and other farming units in the countryside. The *danwei* was established as the standard work unit to which all industrial and white-collar workers as well as any peasant leaving his village must belong.[8]

Even the new tertiary institutions were restructured to fit this basic pattern, with intellectual indoctrination and specialist training being more important there. In this kind of education, centrally planned careers for the graduates were expected to serve the national interest best. A large number of guided specialisations were systematically instituted. The consequent effect on the fragmentation of teaching and learning matched the work cultures that operated on the factory floor. That the consequences would be the suppression of natural talents was known, but this was regarded as a small price to pay if the collective efforts of all could bring rapid development to the country and win the respect of the world.

The mobilisation of the peasantry in China, about half of billion people in the 1950s, to accept a new work culture was an awesome achievement. The *danwei*, or comparable work units in the countryside, were responsible for all training and education, which was structured to transmit a new set of cultural values. These *danwei* were stronger than traditional clan systems and challenged the native-place, family and language group loyalties that had characterised China. Their members depended on the *danwei* for everything they needed. This dependence survived even the internecine struggles of the Cultural Revolution decade and remained the basic framework through which Deng Xiaoping's economic reforms after 1978 had to be implemented.

When the time came to change, their members looked out to see what other Chinese who received different kinds of education elsewhere were doing, especially those in Hong Kong and Taiwan. Indeed, the difference in work cultures inside and outside the mainland was vast. This is not to suggest that there were no dislocations and discontinuities there. What saved those outside was that there was no pretence that there was only one basic kind of work. Thus the environment was much easier for both the surviving Chinese elites and those of peasant origins. For those with elite backgrounds, the educational institutions they looked to were stable and well-structured, and the variety of work they could choose from to suit their specialised talents and skills was greater. As for the peasants who could adapt to the new work cultures, their heritage of internal mobility which had allowed them to take on many kinds of work according to season, or according to need, or according to opportunity, stood them all in good stead. For many, secondary school education became available and was broad enough to reinforce their flexible approaches to new kinds of work.

The Chinese leaders seeking to reform China could see that the educational facilities outside bridged many kinds of work cultures. They looked to the work cultures of Japan and the United States for models, and studied those of the welfare societies of Western Europe, and their British offshoots in Canada and Australasia. The plurality of models may have been confusing, but it was obvious that the presence of choices and the freedom to adopt a work culture that was appropriate to different occupations and professions were assets which these Chinese of whatever origin appreciated and took full advantage of.

Once this was understood, the Chinese within China were ready to change again. This was not easy after thirty years of tightly organised work units which had controlled a narrowly conceived education system. Those who were best adapted to the danwei work culture had the most to unlearn. Although the danwei, or work unit, has survived, the ideal of a single work culture has been abandoned. The plurality of contending forces linked with a market economy, albeit with socialist characteristics, has been accepted. This opened up many new possibilities for the Chinese people. A very elaborate reorganising of formal education, beginning with the tertiary institutions, was undertaken. The peasantry outside the *danwei*, however, did not need this education to respond to the new opportunities. In some areas, like in the Yangzi delta region around Shanghai, agriculture and rural industry was quick to take advantage of the loosening of controls by the central and provincial governments.[9] Thus, when the reforms started after 1978, the most rapid and successful respondents were those outside major cities, especially those who were least tied to state-owned or managed enterprises. These had begun early to act through village and township enterprises that rode on the turmoil of the Cultural Revolution. These were the least structured and benefitted from having links with the rural fold who had retained more of the free-wheeling work cultures of the past.

As the variety of work increased, cadres, workers, peasants and intellectuals alike have responded with different degrees of gusto to the chance to change their attitudes. The results have been dramatic. Gone were the hesitations of the older class of literati whose reluctance to bridge the changes in work cultures had led to their own destruction. Instead, we observe an explosion of pent-up energy as one work culture is eagerly discarded so that people can adopt another that is freer and more variegated. It should not surprise us that the initial outburst came most strongly from the peasant communities of the interior. There the freedom that returned them to their culture of versatility and adaptability was crucial. There are, of course, serious limitations as to how far the majority of those of peasant origins can go without further education to acquire modern skills. But their venturesome vigour has given them a capacity to adapt to new demands with surprising success.

It is remarkable how much of the current work culture in China reminds one of time when the workers of Victorian England organised themselves and gained political respect from their ruling elites. Will the Chinese now proceed to experience what had occurred there? Will they too tame the excesses of capitalist exploitation? Will they form a similarly powerful trade union movement that would lead to the creation of a welfare state mixed economy? There are scholars who expect these things to follow eventually, and comment with dismay on the continuing resistance in China towards efforts to bridge their present work culture with the more humane culture that emerged in Western Europe after World War II. Others dispute that analysis. They suggest that the present regime is building a different kind of bridge, that it does not have to develop towards a Victorian Dickensian past. They are really trying to adapt a select number of capitalist methods to fit the socialist frame that had already been erected, one which it hopes to modify and secure. This shows in the way educational reform has been conducted at all levels, including the universities where a capitalist work culture is still kept at a distance, if not treated as quite unacceptable. The focus there is on providing education which will bridge the different work cultures without threatening the political order.

But the nature of work world-wide is itself facing radical change. With the new technologies changing dramatically each decade, we must all be alert to the probability that the next generation will have to do without the kinds of jobs they are training for. Most will have to prepare themselves for work that has yet to be defined. In that context, the way millions of hardy and versatile Chinese peasants, many already accustomed to lifelong learning, have adapted to dramatic changes to their livelihoods this past century deserve our close attention.

With the advent of new technologies and the evolution of a knowledge-based society as the foundation of the new global economy, profound changes to the nature of work are facing the whole world and not only China. Some speak of a world without regular jobs, a world where work consists of a series of shifting skills and performances to which workers adjust to the best of their ability. As I have shown above with the Chinese, the most carefully trained literati had the greatest difficulty in adapting to radical changes. When they were not given appropriate re-education or re-training conditions, many kicked over the traces and turned their minds to revolution in order to actualise their ideals or regain their past privileges. The less educated peasants, artisans and merchants, in contrast, had the versatility to respond creatively and vigorously once the shock was over. It seems clear that the strong family and clan structure that could be found in any typical Chinese village provided social cohesion, moral support as well as some basic features of a practical education.

As for formal education, especially at the tertiary level, what is appropriate to meet the new challenges has been subject to much scrutiny everywhere of late. Many cherished ways have been questioned. There is increasing awareness that there has been complacency at this high level of education and training, and that over-specialisation is a major weakness in the face of new economic needs. If this continues, how can we talk about empowerment through knowledge and technology?

Open learning is a relatively new area with fewer entrenched values to defend. It is more sensitive to the challenges ahead. It is certainly not overly dominated by a mandarin literati culture that feels that building bridges to connect various kinds of cultures is unnecessary and even beneath its dignity. Therefore, the new forms of distance and lifelong learning may be better placed to provide bridges to the new work cultures that are just being identified. The contrast between Victorian England and post-imperial China may be relevant. The former bridged its strong culture to match the changes that came. The latter resisted and was ultimately forced to self-destruct in order to let a new work culture in. But that China was able to do that, not once but several times in quick succession, owes much to help from its vast human resource base, hundreds of millions from the countryside that prided themselves on their long history of versatility, adaptability and resilience. Not many countries can count on such a resource base, but the experience of flexible responses to changing work cultures has been invaluable. It prepared their people for the new kinds of work that have been identified for our future, and that may be all the empowerment that anyone may need.

Notes

1. The pioneering work edited by Asa Briggs, *Chartist Studies*, London: Macmillan, 1959, remains a classic. The range of his contributions to our understanding of how people responded to the changing nature of modern working conditions may be found in the first three volumes of *The Collected Essays of Asa Briggs*. Brighton: Harvester Press, 1985–1991. I have taken the phrase "serious pursuits" from the subtitle of his third volume, *Serious Pursuits: Communications and Education*. From *The Nineteenth Century: The Contradictions of Progress*. London: Thames and Hudson, 1985, which he edited, I have borrowed his phrase "contradictions of progress".

2. Braudel, *Civilization and Capitalism*, *15th-18th Centuries*, olume two: *The Wheels of Commerce*. Translated by Sian Reynold., Berkeley: University of California Press, 1992, pp. 255–256.

3. Asa Briggs. *Victorian People: Some Reassessments of People, Institutions, Ideas and Events, 1851–1967.* London: Odhams Press, 1954. And also his subsequesnt study, *Victorian Cities.* London: Odhams Press, 1963.

4. For a broad survey, Lynn Pan. *Sons of the Yellow Emperor: The Story of the Overseas Chinese.* London: Secker & Warburg, 1990, provides a most readable introduction to the subject. More details may be found in the *Encyclopedia of the Chinese Overseas*, which she edited, published in Singapore by Archipelago Press and Landmark Books, 1998.

5. Ruth Hayhoe. *China's Universities, 1895–1995: A Century of Cultural Conflict.* New York: Garland Publishers, 1996. Also Yeh Wen-Hsin. *The Alienated Academy: Culture and Politics in Republican China, 1919–1937.* Cambridge, Mass.: Center of East Asian Studies, Harvard University, 1990.

6. R.H. Tawney. *Land and Labour in China.* Londoon: G. Allen & Unwin, 1932.

7. Philip C. Huang. *The Peasant Economy and Social Change in North China.* Stanford: Stanford University Press, 1985; and Ramon Myers. *The Chinese Peasant Economy: Agricultural Development in Hopei and Shantung, 1890–1949.* Cambridge, Mass.: Harvard University Press, 1970.

8. Lu Xiaobo and Elizabeth J. Perry. Eds. *Danwei: The Changing Chinese Workplace in Historical and Comparative Perspectives.* Armonk, N.Y.: M.E. Sharpe, 1997. Also Andrew G. Walder. *Communist Neo-traditionalism: Work and Authority in Chinese Industry.* Berkeley: University of California Press, 1986.

9. Lynn T. White. *Unstately Power*, volume I: *Local Causes of China's Economic Reforms.* Armonk, N.Y.: M.E. Sharpe, 1998.

Index

Adriatic Sea   139
Africa   102–3
Afro-American   55
Aiguo   18, 20
America   3, 43, 78, 85, 104,
  111–2, 120–1, 124–5, 140–1
American Civil War   2, 121, 123,
  125
Aminuddin Baki   62n
Amyot, Jacques   60n
Anarchism   33
Ang See, Teresita   57
Angkor Wat   98
Anglo-American   81, 84, 91, 133
Anglo-Chinese   76, 82
Anglo-Indian (forces)   3
Anglo-Japanese alliance   85
Anti-Semites   54
ANU (Australian National
  University)   37, 46, 47, 121
Arabs   17, 55, 98–100, 103, 124,
  133
Armenian   55

ASEAN   30
Asia-Pacific   51
Assimilation   18, 41, 47, 54
Atlantic Ocean   102
Australasia   3, 17, 20, 30, 38, 43,
  46, 48–9, 51, 54, 107–9, 111–2,
  119, 121, 124, 134, 140

Babylonian empire   121
Baltic (peoples)   16–17
Baltic Sea   138
Bamboo slips (writing)   121
Bandung   108
Bangkok   53
Batavia   102, 108
Beijing   3, 21–2, 56, 71, 84, 89
Benda, Harry   41, 61n
Bengali   133
Biographical literature   125
Borneo   100, 134
Borobodur   98
Braudel, Fernand   139

Brazil   134
Briggs, Asa   129–30, 136, 139,
    148n
Britain (British)   13, 16, 18, 26–9,
    40, 44, 46, 73, 75, 78–81, 84–5,
    89, 91, 102–4, 109, 111–2, 125,
    136, 138, 144
Brooke family   26
Buddhism   8, 98, 116, 133
Bugis   103
Burma   108–9, 111, 135
Business (Commerce)   3, 5, 9,
    24–5, 31, 35, 43, 47, 50, 53,
    65n, 80–1, 90–1, 93, 95, 97–104,
    132, 135
Butterfield & Swire   87

Caesar, Julius   120
Cambodia   40
Cambridge   81
Canada   134, 144
Canberra   47, 121
Canton, see Guangzhou
Cantonese   42, 79, 85, 87
Capitalism   4, 6, 24–5, 49, 53,
    71, 78, 91–2, 94, 102–3, 116,
    118–9, 135, 137, 139, 141, 146
Catholic   18
Central Asia   3
Central China   111, 113
Champa   100–1
Chaozhou, see Teochiu
Chartists   139
Chauvinism   51
Chen Da   40
Cheng Ho, see Zheng He

Chiang Kai-shek   8, 22, 90, 92
Chin Kee Onn   114
Chin Peng   28, 62n
China Coast   3
China Relief Fund   113
Chinese diaspora, The   38
Chinese Southern Diaspora Centre
    37, 58
Christianity   8, 116, 133
Citizen   18, 45
Civic Society   9
Civil rights   54
Civil Service   25
Civil War   16–7, 28, 33, 44, 76,
    114, 125, 137, 141
Civilisation & Capitalism   139
Clan (associations)   53, 143, 147
Clausewitz   120
Cohen, Abner   52
Cold War   10, 12, 17, 22, 114,
    118–9
Colombo Plan   108
Commonwealth   129
Communism, Communist Party
    5–8, 12, 16–7, 19–20, 22, 24–5,
    27–9, 31–3, 35, 40
(Chinese)   44, 78, 85, 89–90, 94,
    113, 115–6, 119, 137, 142
Confrontation   29
Confucian State   2, 4, 8
Confucianism   8, 75, 115–6,
    118–9, 121, 123–4, 133, 141
Conservatism   13
Coppel, Charles   49, 65n
Cornell (University)   40, 48–9
Corruption   6, 9, 34, 115, 122
Croats   17

Crusades 120
Cultural Revolution 8, 12, 22–3, 25, 30, 46–7, 49, 143, 145
Cushman, Jennifer 37
Czechs 16, 41

Danwei (work units) 143–5
Darwinian 135
Democracy 7, 12–3, 33
Deng Xiaoping 9–10, 31, 35, 51, 116–7, 137, 143
Diaoyutai 22
Diaspora 16–7, 38, 41, 51–7
Disney, Walt 122
Dunlop, Sir Edward 'Weary' 107–9, 115, 119–20, 126
Dutch 18, 28, 40–1, 100–2, 104

East Asia 100
East China Sea 22
East India Company 102
East Timor 23
Ebury, Sue 108
Education 47, 50, 74, 79–80, 89, 129–32, 140–6
Elites 3, 5–8, 10, 12–3, 74, 94, 103, 117, 140–3, 144, 146
Elliott, Alan 59n
Emergency (Malaya) 28
Encyclopedia of the Chinese overseas 57
English 18, 20, 38, 42, 44, 55, 69n, 74, 79–81, 111–2
English Civil War 125
Entreprenuers 3, 53, 97–8, 135, 141

Environment 136
"Essential outsiders" 53, 68n
Ethnic Chinese, see huaren
Eurasian 44, 77, 92
Europe 4, 16–7, 28, 41–3, 86, 88, 100–2, 109–10, 114, 120, 125, 138–9, 140

Federated Malay States 42
Fengjian 121
Finance 3, 4, 10, 52, 93
Firth, Raymond 59n
FitzGerald, Stephen 49
France 16, 18, 40, 85, 102–3, 111, 125, 139
Freedman, Maurice 40–1, 47, 59n, 60n, 64n
Fujian, also see Hokkien

Germany 5, 16, 41
Goa 102
Gorbachev 116
Great Depression 91
Great Leap Forward 8, 30
Greek 38, 55
Guangdong 99, 113
Guangzhou 3, 84, 88, 93
Guomindang 8, 15, 20–1, 23, 33, 56, 90, 113, 115, 126

Hainanese 42
Hakka 42
Han (dynasty) 123
Hanoi 32
Hatta Mohammed 104

Hawaii   32, 86
Hebrew   38
Heritage   8, 32
High Noon   123
Hinduism   98, 133
History   7, 8, 16, 39, 42, 45–6, 48, 59n, 95, 131
Hitler   16
Ho Kai   86, 94
Hokkien   42, 79
Holocaust   41, 54
Homer, Iliad   120, 123
Hong Kong   15, 19, 24, 32, 41, 48–53, 56–7, 67n, 71–95, 104, 107, 118, 144
Hotung, Sir Robert   77, 82
Hu Liyuan   86, 94
Hua Mulan   122
Huang, Philip   142
Huaqiao   15, 17–20, 28, 31–4, 36, 39–45, 51–2
Huaren   18, 31–6, 39, 57
Huayi   18, 31–6, 39, 57
Human rights   13, 54, 56, 117
Hundred Flowers   8
Hundred Years War   125

Ibans   134
Identity, identities   4, 7
Ideology   5, 21–2, 28, 33, 78, 116, 118
Indian Ocean   100
Indians   17, 28, 42, 44, 55, 97–9, 101–3, 133
Indigenous people   35

IndoChinese states   50, 59n
Indonesia   21, 24–5, 29–30, 40–1, 46, 49–50, 56, 61n, 98, 133, 135
Industrial revolution   131
Industry   3, 5, 43, 50, 93, 103, 140
"informal empires"   53
Inglis, Ken   121
Institute of Southeast Asian Studies   61n
Integration   49, 54
Intelligentsia   28, 31
Ipoh   32, 42, 44
Iranians   17, 55
Irish   16, 55
Islam   98, 116, 133
Israel   17, 55
ISSCO, International Society for the Study of the Chinese Overseas   57, 70n
Italy   5, 16, 55

Jakarta   108
Japan   4, 5, 11, 16–7, 20, 22m, 27–8, 33, 39, 43, 50–1, 62n, 77, 84–6, 91, 101, 104, 107, 110–5, 118–9, 125, 135, 141, 144
Java   99, 100–1, 108
Jews   16, 38, 41, 53–4, 68n
Jiang, Joseph P.   67n
Jiangnan Arsenal   88
Jinan University   40, 59n
Jindaishi Yanjiu   127n
Joint Declaration   80
Josephus   120
Judaeo-Christian   133

Kadazans 134
Kang Youwei 33, 61n
Keating, Paul 107
Khmer empire 100
Kinta 42
Kintok Mountains 109
Kobe 32
Korea 51, 104, 114, 118
Kuala Lumpur 32, 42, 47
Kunshan 87
Kuomintang, see Guomindang
Kurds 17

Law 3–4, 9, 13
Lee, Robert E 2
Legge, James 87
Lenin 28, 35
Li Changfu 39
Li Hongzhang 8
Liberalism 6, 12, 33, 117
Lim, Linda 51
Lincoln 1, 2
Liu Shimu 39
London 40, 48
Luodi Shenggen 38, 58n

Macau 15, 19, 84m, 86–8, 93, 102
Mackie, Jamie 49, 65n
Mahabharata 98
Majapahit 100
Malacca 42, 102
Malay archipelago 99, 103–4
Malay peninsula 100, 102, 108

Malaya, Malaysia 23, 26–30, 35, 42, 44–7, 49, 61n, 101, 104, 111–2, 114, 133–4
Malayan Communist Party 28, 113, 115
Malayan People's Anti-Japanese Army 113
Manchu 3–4, 11, 31, 74, 88–9, 124
Manchuria 91
Mandarin 116
Manila 57, 70n, 85, 102
Mao Zedong 7–9, 12, 30–1, 34–5, 46, 51, 56, 87, 92–3, 117, 137
Market economy 9, 10, 13, 25, 35, 72
Marx 20, 28, 35
Maspero, Henri 59n
May Fourth Movement 90
May Thirtieth incident 90
Media 23, 33, 43, 117–8
Medical College for Chinese 74
Mediterranean 101
Melbourne 53
"Melting-pot" 54
Menam Valley 99
Mercantilism 102
Mexico 134
Middle-class 28
Migration 3, 38, 53, 56
Minangkabau 103
Ming (dynasty) 100–1
Minority 18, 21, 38, 49, 53
Missionary 11, 23, 141
Modernism 7

Mongol   11, 100, 124
Multiculturalism   54
Muslim (rebellions)   2–3, 38, 61n,
    99–100
Myanmar, see Burma
Myers, Ramon   142

Nanhai trade   45
Nanjing   16, 21, 44, 62n, 74, 90,
    113, 115
Nanyang   45
Nanyang xuehui   40, 59n
Naples   139
Napoleon   103
Nation-building   7, 21, 27, 30, 41,
    44–5, 49, 54, 126, 134
Nationalism   6, 27, 31–3, 35, 39,
    41–4, 54, 75–6, 78, 85–6, 88–9,
    91, 93, 114–5, 120
Nationalists   12, 15, 20, 63n,
    90–1, 113–4
Nationals   18, 22
Native-place society   53, 143
Nazi   41
New Guinea   111
New Spain   120
New York   22
Newell, William   60n
Ng Choy, see Wu Ting-fang
North America   17, 19–20, 22–3,
    30, 48, 51, 54–5, 86
North China   111, 113
North Sea   138

Old Testament   121

Open learning   129–32, 147
Oracle bones   121
Orthodoxy   9
Overseas Chinese, see huaqiao
Oxford   81

Pacific War   18, 20, 27, 33, 110,
112
Pakistani   55
Palestine   16
Pan, Lynn   57, 149n
"Pariah entrepreneurs"   53
Paris   84
Patriotism   18, 20, 22, 33, 49, 56,
    80, 122
Pearl Harbour   112
Peasants   137–49
Pelliot, Paul   59n
Peloponnesian War   120
Penang   32, 102
People's Liberation Army   114
Perak   42
Persia   98, 124, 133
Philippines   18, 21–2, 40, 100,
    104
Pluralism   9, 12, 13, 57
Populism   3
Portuguese   40, 84, 100–1
Professionals   9, 10
Proletariat   28, 35, 46
Purcell, Victor   40, 59n
Pye, Lucian   60n

Qing (dynasty)   1–2, 12, 15, 56,
    61n, 74–5, 88, 124, 141

racism   19, 39, 54
Ramayana   98
rebellions   2–3, 7, 122
Redding, Gordon   53
reform   7, 9–10, 12–3, 34, 39
Reid, Anthony   37, 39, 67n
republic   4–5, 8, 15, 22–3, 33, 74, 89
Revisionism   52
revolution   6–8, 13, 15–36, 39, 49, 76, 115
Robison, Richard   51
Roman (empire)   120
Russia   3, 5, 16, 31, 78

Sabah   26, 29
Saigon   32, 85
San Francisco   32, 57
San Guo (Three Kingdoms)   122
Sanskritic culture   133
Sarawak   26, 29
schools   9, 33, 42–3, 79–80, 130, 132, 140–2, 144
Science   3, 9, 76, 87, 131
Scottish Highlands War   125
self-determination   11–12
Shandong   91
Shanghai   3, 76–80, 83–95, 145
Shengshi weiyan   87
Short history of the Nanyang Chinese, A   45
Shuihu Zhuan (Water Margin)   122
Shum Chun (river)   94
Siam, see Thailand
Sima Qian   121
Singapore   23, 26–7, 29–30, 40, 42, 44, 46, 49–50, 53, 55, 59n, 83, 104, 112, 114, 116–8
Skinner, G. William   40, 47, 60n, 64n
Small Dagger rebellion   85
Social Darwinism   4
Social welfare   80
socialism   9, 24, 28, 36, 45, 72, 146
Sojourners & Settlers   37
sojourners, see huaqiao
Sojourning   38, 45
Song (dynasty)   100, 123
South Africa   23
South Asia   98–100
South China   82, 88, 140
South China Sea   100
South Pacific   111
Southeast Asia   3, 18–9, 21–3, 26, 28, 30, 38, 40, 42–3, 46, 48, 50–1, 56, 97–104, 111–2, 114, 140
sovereignty   11
Soviet Union   16, 23, 30, 114, 116, 118
Span   40, 100–2
Spring & Autumn Annuals   121
Srivijaya   100
Stalin   7, 35
students   35
Suharto   25, 50
Sukarno   21, 24–5, 29, 46, 104
Sumatra   100
Sun Yat-sen   15, 18, 31–3, 35, 61n, 73–5, 82, 86–9, 94
Sun Zi   123
Surabaya   42
Suryadinata, Leo   49, 60n, 65n
Sweden   138

Tacitus   120
Taiping rebellion   2–3, 85
Taiwan   11, 15, 19, 21–4, 28, 31–2, 41–3, 79–80, 130, 132, 140–2, 144
Tan Chee Beng   60n
Tan Kah Kee   114
Tan, Antonio   60n
Tan, Mely   60n
Tang (dynasty)   123
Taoism   8, 133
Tawney, R.H.   142
technology   4, 8, 47, 52–3, 87, 129, 132, 136, 139, 146–7
Teochiu   42, 79
Thailand   18, 40, 60n, 101, 104, 108–9, 135
Thucydides   120–1, 123
Tian Jukang   40, 59n
Tiananmen   80, 118
Tianjin   3
Topley, Marjorie   59n
Trade unions   80, 139, 146
trade, see business
Tsai, Shih-shan, Henry   61n
Turkic, Turkish   17, 124, 133

"Ungrounded empires"   53, 68n
United Nations   20, 22, 31
United States   2–4, 10-11, 17, 21–3, 28, 30, 54, 84, 114, 134, 144
unity   11–2
university   40, 130, 132, 141, 143, 146–7

University of Hong Kong   74, 81, 86
University of Malaya   44, 63n
Urdu   133

Van der Post, Sir Laurens   109–10, 125
Vancouver   32, 53
Victorian England   139, 146m, 148
Vietnam   17, 30, 46, 49, 99, 102

Wang Ling-chi   38, 57
Wang Tao   87, 94
War Memorial   121
Warring states   121
Weightman, George   60n
Wen Xiongfei   39
West Asia   98, 100
West, Westerners   4–6, 8, 10–1, 13, 17, 32, 45, 50, 53, 55, 71, 74–5, 78, 81, 88, 92, 101, 103, 113, 115, 117–20, 126, 132–3, 135, 141, 144, 146
Wickberg,Edgar   60n, 61n
Willmott, Donald   60n
Willmott, Wlliam   60n
workers   3, 28, 139
World Entrepreneurs Convention   53, 68n
World Huaren Federation   69n
World War II   16–7, 26, 54, 92, 110, 125, 146
Wu Ting-fang   73–4, 82
Wuxia (armed knights) novels   122

Xinjiang   3
Xu Yunqiao   40, 59n

Yangtse valley, see Yangzi
Yangzi   95, 145
Yao Nan   40
"Yellow peril"   51
Yen Ching-hwang   49, 61n, 64n
Yokohama   32
Yong, C.F.   49, 65n
Yoshihara, Kunio   51

Yuan (dynasty)   100, 124
Yuan Shikai   8
Yugoslavia   17

Zhang Liqian   40
Zhang Zhidong   8
Zhejiang   99
Zheng Guanying   87, 94
Zheng He   45, 100
Zionist   16
Zongli yamen   1